BALTI

ESTONIA · LATVIA · LITHUANIA

Claude Hervé-Bazin

JPMGUIDES

Contents

ESTONIA

This Way Estonia

Pride Regained

Surrounded by such powerful neighbours as the Scandinavians, Russia and, till not too long ago, the Germans, the Estonians must have had indomitable strength of character to keep their national identity intact. Proof that it has succeeded is there in Estonia's blue, black and white flag flying on public buildings.

With an area of 45,227 sq km, Estonia is the smallest of the Baltic States. It borders Latvia to the north and opens onto the Baltic to the west, breaking up into a scattering of 1,521 isles and islets. Helsinki, across the Gulf of Finland to the north, is 80 km from Tallinn, the Estonian capital. To the east, the River Narva and the great Lake Peïpous (3,555 sq km) mark the frontier with Russia. The territory is largely flat, with wooded hills to the south, interspersed with peat bogs, swampy hollows and countless lakes. At 318 m, Suur Munamägi, is the highest point of all three Baltic States. The core features of Estonia's identity are the forests, which cover 40 per cent of the land, and the rural landscapes with farms isolated in the midst of vast clearings. The national parks and nature reserves are home to wolf, bear, lynx, deer, otter and wild boar.

Of the 1.3 million inhabitants, only 68% are true Estonians, the rest being Russian (26%) and minorities from other former Soviet republics (5%), who immigrated after Estonia's forced annexation to the Soviet Union in 1944. The Russian-speaking community represents 98% of the town of Narva and nearly half of Tallinn's population. The Old Believers (traditional Orthodox *raskolniki*), who settled around Lake Peïpous after fleeing Russia in the 18th century, have gained ready acceptance. To the south live the Setus, of Finnish origin, who adopted the Orthodox religion when they were absorbed in the Russian Empire. The Germans, for centuries the dominant class among landowners, left at the end of World War II, as did the Swedes living since the 13th century on the Baltic coast and islands.

Estonia has known barely 30 years of independence in 7 centuries. Yet no war, no invader has succeeded in undermining its national cohesion. The Tallinn Choral Festival still re-enacts the "Singing Revolution" that heralded the fracture of Soviet power.

Flashback

Early times	People of Finno-Ugric stock, tribes migrating from beyond the Urals, settle in the present-day Baltic States around 8000 BC. From there, they go on to settle Finland.
9th–11th centuries AD	United against Viking invaders, the Estonian ancestors known to Romans as Aestii set up their main trading centre in the 10th century on the coast of the Gulf of Finland. Russia, ruled from Kiev, seizes the southwest of the country in 1030.
12th–16th centuries	In 1202 the Pope calls for a Northern Crusade against the pagan peoples of the Baltic. Albert von Appeldorn, Bishop of Riga, founds the Order of the Sword Brethren to conquer southern Estonia while King Waldemar II of Denmark seizes the north. He takes over the town of Tallinn ("Danish Fortress") in 1219. By 1290, Estonian resistance is quelled. Meanwhile, Tallinn (known as Reval) has joined the Hanseatic League (1248) and trade is flourishing. In 1343, though the peasant revolt of the "Night of St George" is brutally crushed, it precipitates the end of Danish power. The country is bought off and passes into the hands of the Teutonic Knights, who rule there until 1561.
16th–17th centuries	While the Teutonic Knights give way and the Hanseatic League gradually breaks up, Estonia falls prey to the territorial ambitions of its neighbours. Joining the Reformation, the country is torn asunder by the Livonian War (1558–83) unleashed by Ivan the Terrible. Finally, it passes into the hands of the Swedes. In practice, however, Estonia remains under the control of the "Baltic Barons", Germanic landowners. The country is unified in 1645 after the Swedes buy the island of Saaremaa, briefly a Danish possession.
18th–19th centuries	In course of the Northern Wars opposing Sweden and Russia, Peter the Great seizes Estonia in 1710—formally ratified by the Treaty of Nystad in 1721. Swedish reforms are scrapped and Estonian peasants reduced to the status of serfs. The Baltic Barons hold on to their power position. In the second half of the 19th century, Estonian national sen-

timent revives, with Tsar Alexander III trying to stifle it by a campaign of Russification. The opening of a railway link to Saint Petersburg (1879) contributes to a new economic prosperity. Tallinn becomes one of the main ports in the Russian Empire.

20th century–present

On February 24, 1918, in the wake of the Russian Revolution, Estonia proclaims its independence. The announcement of agrarian reforms contrary to the interests of the Baltic Barons provokes immediate German intervention. A few months later, the Russians take over. In February 1920, after signing a peace treaty, Estonia enters the League of Nations, but this proves to be a short-lived adventure. Occupied in June 1940 by Stalin's troops under the terms of the German-Soviet Pact and annexed two months later, Estonia is invaded by German troops in 1941 and forced to side with Hitler's army. The country is bombarded, recaptured by the Soviets, purged and subjected to a mass exodus, ending with Estonia's formal incorporation in the Soviet Union. The Forest Brothers resistance movement continues for several years. In 1949, nearly 80,000 peasants are deported to Siberia. Heavily industrialized, Estonia maintains the highest standard of living of all the states in the Soviet Union.

At the end of the 1980s, the Estonians step up the pressure to reaffirm their autonomy. The opportunity finally arises with the break-up of the Soviet Union, and the country declares itself an independent republic August 20, 1991. In April 2004, Estonia becomes a member of NATO and a month later joins the European Union.

On the Scene

Any visit to Estonia begins naturally enough with the vibrant medieval city of Tallinn on the Gulf of Finland. Especially in summer, its picturesque Old Town is exuberantly alive with all sorts of festivals and concerts.

Just 40 km east of the Estonian capital are the magnificent landscapes of the Lahemaa National Park. To the west are the huge Lake Peïpous and the university town of Tartu. The southeast of the country is covered with dense forest, while the west coast offers excursions out to the islands of Hiiumaa and Saaremaa.

➡ TALLINN
Lower Town, Toompea Hill, Kadriorg,
Rocca al Mare, Beaches

Inhabited since the end of the 10th century, Tallinn made its first documented appearance under the name of Koluvan on a map drawn in 1154 by the Arab geographer Muhammad al-Idrisi. A few decades later, in the summer of 1219, the town was conquered along with the rest of northern Estonia by King Waldemar II of Denmark. The fortifications built on Toompea Hill gave the town its name—*Tani linn*, "Danish Fortress". Taken in 1227 by the Knights of the Sword Brethren (who merged with the Teutonic Knights ten years later), then returned to the Danes in 1238, the town joined the Hanseatic League in 1248. The purchase of the country by the Teutonic Knights in 1346 prompted an important new influx of German merchants and craftsmen. Furs, leather and seal blubber were exported to the Baltic ports while herring, wines and salt were imported for the Russian Empire. The Swedish invasion of 1561 marked the beginning of a long economic decline, worsened by the rise in regional conflicts. As a Russian state, Tallinn rediscovered its energy with the

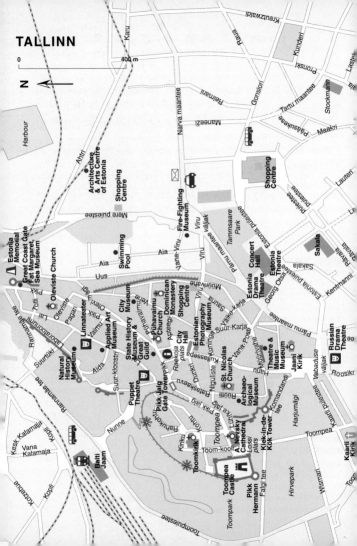

arrival of the railways in 1870. Its industrialization grew with Estonia's incorporation in the Soviet Union in 1944. The population doubled over the following 15 years, and today nearly half its 400,000 inhabitants are Russian-speaking.

Three different parts make up the city of Tallinn: the Old Town (Vanallin) forming the kernel; the new town built in the 19th century, and the suburban belt of the Soviet era. Declared a UNESCO World Heritage Site in 1997 after its restoration was completed, the Old Town is divided between the citadel on Toompea Hill and the lower town centred on Town Hall Square *(Raekoja plats)*. Cobblestone lanes thread through a confusion of medieval roofs, pepperpot turrets and church spires. The Old Town is largely surrounded by ramparts; 2.5 km in length, they were among the most formidable in northern Europe. Of the 46 towers and bastions, 26 are still standing.

As the setting for the White Nights in June, the site attracts hordes of summer visitors, especially from Finland. Hydrofoils cross the gulf from Helsinki in 90 minutes. All through summer, against a backdrop of boutiques and pavement cafés, concerts and festivals exemplified by the Tallinn Old Town Days bring the aura of another age to the streets.

Lower Town

Throughout the Middle Ages, the Lower Town, where the German merchants and craftsmen set up shop, maintained a fairly broad autonomy with regard to the Teu-

VANA TOOMAS

Tallinn used to organize archery contests for aristocrats in medieval times. The target was a wooden or iron bird perched on the Town Hall's spire. One year, none of the contestants managed to hit it. It was then that a young boy, Thomas, pushed his way out from the crowd of spectators, flexed his bow, aimed and hit the target. The Mayor took his defense against the rebukes of the nobles, and made sure he was given special archery training. Thomas became one of the most skilful guards at the gates of Tallinn.

Today, the city's night-owls may confirm another legend: now and again an old man emerges from Lake Ulemiste to see if the town has been completed. Vana Toomas invariably replies that it will still take a good few years. Grumbling to himself, the old fellow goes away again. If ever Vana Toomas were to say the work was done, the waters of the lake would flood the town.

The domes, spires and rooftops of Tallinn's charming Old Town.

tonic Knights up on the Toompea citadel. Old Tallinn owes them much of its charm: warehouses, Gothic dwellings, openwork doors and gates, Gothic and Baroque churches. Almost entirely closed off to traffic, the centre has become delightful area for walking. The traditional entrance is from the east, through the Viru Gate. It once stood 13 m high and has preserved part of its arcades and several stone turrets.

Town Hall

Originally the market square, Town Hall Square *(Raekoja plats)* has been the city's centre for seven centuries. It is sur-

rounded by pastel-coloured façades and pavement cafés. Set sturdily on the southern side of the square, the Town Hall *(Raekoja)* dates back to 1404, and is considered the oldest secular Gothic edifice in Northern Europe. Its slender spire is topped by a weathervane in the shape of a medieval warrior known as Vana Toomas (Old Thomas); today's statue is the second replacement of the original, which was set in place in 1503.

The Town Hall interior is open to the public Monday to Friday for guided tours (reservation necessary), unless official municipal business is in session. Highlights are the Citizens Hall with its superb vaulted ceiling and the Magistrates Council Room, furnished with finely carved 14th-century wooden benches.

Around the Square

At Raekoja plats 6, in the narrow lane running behind the Town Hall, the old 14th-century prison has been converted into the national Photography Museum *(Raevangla Fotomuuseum)*.

On the north side of the square at No. 11 is one of Europe's oldest municipal pharmacies *(Raeapteek)*, open for business back in 1422. One small room displays ancient and impressive pharmaceutical instruments.

Nearby, a large L formed by two long paving-stones marks the spot where a priest was executed in the 17th century for having murdered with an axe a tavern waitress who served him a bad omelette.

Church of the Holy Ghost

Beside the pharmacy, a narrow arcaded passage leads to the Church of the Holy Ghost *(Pühavaimu Kirik)*, built at the end of the 14th century by the Order of the same name. On the façade facing Pikk Street is a splendid clock, Tallinn's oldest (1648). Inside the church, each of the twin naves is edged by a wooden gallery decorated with painted scenes from the Bible and carved bas-relief figures and demons' heads. Note, too, the richly carved Renaissance pulpit and Baroque pews. The altar triptych (1483) is the work of German artist Bernt Notke. Classical music concerts are held here on most Mondays at 6 p.m.

Pikk Street

Several handsome medieval dwellings distinguish this street leading to the harbour. At No. 17, push open the heavy doors decorated with lion-headed knockers, emblematic of the Great Guild

---

MEDIEVAL GUILDS

In the Baltic States, as in all medieval Europe, powerful associations were formed from the corporations of craftsmen and merchants from the 14th century. Among them were the Brotherhood of Black Heads and the Guild of St Canut, bringing together from 1326 "noble" artisans such as goldsmiths, bakers, tailors and shoemakers, most of them German. In 1341, the Guild of St Olaf *(Oleviste)* appeared, opening up to more humble trades—butchers, furriers and tanners. The guilds disappeared in 1877 with the enactment of a new Russian urban law.

Hall, the most important in medieval Tallinn. The Gothic building (1410) today houses the Estonian History Museum *(Eeste Ajaloomuuseum)* tracing the nation's story from prehistoric times to the Middle Ages. At Nos. 24–26 are the seats of the St Olaf Guild and the Brotherhood of the Black Heads (closed to the public). The latter was founded in 1399 by bachelor merchants who sought the protection of St Maurice, a Moor whose colour gave their association its name. Altered in 1597 to its present Renaissance style, the superb façade is decorated with bas-reliefs of the coats of arms of Bruges, Novgorod, London and Bergen (the Hanseatic League's four major *Kontors*, or trading posts) and a fine series of saints and knights.

Warehouses

In Lai Street, parallel to Pikk Street, you'll see several typical medieval warehouses with slender silhouettes and, in some cases, their hoisting-beam still jutting out from the wall. No. 23 is among the best restored of the buildings. No. 17 houses the collections of the Estonian Applied Arts Museum *(Tarbekunstimuuseum)* covering the period from

Closed door: that of the seat of the Brotherhood of Blackheads.

the 1920s to the present day; it stages interesting temporary exhibitions.

St Olaf's Church

The upper end of Lai Street is overwhelmed by the formidable mass of St Olaf's Church *(Oleviste Kirik)*, dedicated to King Olaf II of Norway and built by an unknown architect also named Olaf. Legend has it that he fell to his death from the church tower. First mentioned in 1267, the church is crowned by a spire 124 m high. Its height made it suitable for the KGB's radio antenna during Soviet rule. The present interior, after frequent fires over the centuries, dates back to the 1840s.

Fat Margaret

Just behind other medieval warehouses at the bottom of Pikk Street are the Sea Gates bearing the town's coats of arms. Built into the ramparts in the early 16th century, the Fat Margaret *(Paks Margareeta)* artillery tower now houses the Marine Museum *(Meremuuseum)*. There's a fine view from the top of the tower, particularly over the city walls themselves. In a small park just outside the fortifications, within view of the ferry port's smokestacks, is a monument commemorating the 842 victims of the *Estonia* ferry shipwrecked in 1994 between Sweden and Tallinn.

13

Dominican Monastery

Double back to St Olaf's Church and take the lane opposite leading down to Vene Street. At No. 16, near the ruins of St Catherine's Church, is a door leading to the Dominican monastery *(Dominiiklaste Klooster)*. Founded in 1246, this remained an important centre for the dissemination of Christian thought until the Reformation. It now displays a collection of stone sculptures from the 15th and 16th centuries.

City Museum

At Vene Street 17, the fascinating City Museum *(Tallinna Linnamuuseum)* is housed in a superbly restored merchant's residence of the 14th century. Its collections and reconstructions trace the history of Tallinn and the life of its citizens from their beginnings to the present time. Among the exhibits, see the splendid models of ships belonging to the Brotherhood of the Black Heads, the executioner's mighty sword and objects from everyday life under the Soviets, including a carpet woven with the portrait of Mikhail Kalinin, Stalin's puppet head of state. You will also see the second version of Vana Toomas (Old Thomas) in full armour with a big hat on his head and bristling moustache; this figure was in place on top of the Town Hall from 1953 to 1998.

St Nicholas' Church

South of Raekoja plats in the oldest part of the Lower Town, among more medieval warehouses, is the Gothic St Nicholas' Church *(Niguliste,* 13th–15th centuries). It now houses the Museum of Medieval Art, which includes in its outstanding collections a fragment of German artist Bernt Notke's celebrated 15th-century *Dance of Death* and an altarpiece by Hermann Rode (1482).

The nearby Archaeology Museum at Rüütli Street 10 is undergoing renovation.

Toompea Hill

This is where the city was founded. An Estonian bastion from the 10th century, then the seat of foreign power (Danish, German, Swedish), the great limestone crag rising on the northwest corner of the Lower Town lived for many years independently off its surroundings. For centuries, access was possible only via one long sloping street passing through the Pikk jalg gate (1380). In 1454, the lords of the Upper Town decided to close the street each evening to barricade themselves against the sporadic revolts of the "Lower" citizens.

Castle Square

Castle Square *(Lossi plats)* runs alongside the monumental onion-bulb domed Russian Orthodox Alexander Nevski Cathedral, symbol of the tsarist Russification at the end of the 19th century.

Opposite, the Baroque Toompea Castle *(Toompea Loss)* with its pink and white façade is now the seat of government and Estonia's Parliament (closed to the public).

Fortifications

Though nothing remains of the first castle built here in 1219 by King Waldemar II of Denmark, you can still see three of four towers in the ramparts erected by the knights of the Sword Brotherhood. The highest, 46 m tall, is Pikk Herman, dating from 1371; it looms over the garden next to the castle entrance.

Lower down, the town's biggest artillery tower (1483) is built into the fortifications: its commanding position looking down at the private homes of the Lower Town earned it the German dialect nickname *Kiek in de Kök* (Peep Into the Kitchen). Its spiral staircase leads to rooms on six floors forming a handsome museum of Tallinn history from the 12th to the 17th centuries, with a military emphasis on weapons, fortification models and maps.

Still lodged in the outer walls are nine cannonballs fired by the troops of Ivan the Terrible during the war of Livonia (present-day Estonia plus part of Latvia).

Cathedral Church

North of Castle Square is one of Estonia's oldest churches, founded in 1232. Now Lutheran, the Cathedral Church *(Toomkirik)* was originally Gothic but has been frequently modified, particularly after the fire of 1684. The tower dates from 1779. Inside are several carved or otherwise elaborate marble tombs of nobles and military heroes, a fine Baroque pulpit (1686) and various coats of arms.

SONG FESTIVAL

Near Kadriorg Park east of Tallinn are the grounds and open-air amphitheatre where the renowned Tallinn Song Festival is held every 5 years (the next one is scheduled for 2008). The tradition dates back to the 19th century and, spurred on by the progressive movement of Gorbachev's *perestroika*, it culminated in 1988 and 1989 with the participation of nearly 300,000 people singing their hearts out for national independence. The country's strong choral tradition is also sustained by an annual spring festival held in churches and concert halls around Tallinn.

15

Belvedere

From the rear of the church, take Kohtu Street up to a viewpoint affording a beautiful panorama of the city, with St Olaf's tower and the port to the west, the Town Hall and its spire to the right, and in the foreground the gate of Pikk jalg.

Museum of Estonian Art

The Kumu—as the *Kunstimuuseum* is called—is installed in an ultramodern building near Kadriorg Park, is devoted to Estonian painting and sculpture from the 18th century to the present day. The museum also stages temporary exhibitions of international contemporary artists.

Kadriorg

Following his conquest of Estonia, Peter the Great had a summer palace built at Kadriorg, surrounded by a vast park; today it is one of Tallinn's most popular recreation areas. The Baroque design by an Italian architect was completed in 1725. Many of the rooms are now give over to the highly regarded Museum of Foreign Art *(Kadrioru Kunstimuusem)*. A highlight of the collection is a group of Flemish paintings from the 16th to 18th centuries. Also noteworthy is the beautiful 2nd-floor room with inlaid wood panelling and a fine display of china and porcelain.

Mikkeli Museum

Across the street from the palace, this museum is renowned for its collection of Russian icons, the oldest dating back to the early 16th century. Upstairs is a collection of European paintings and lithographs (including several Rembrandts) and European and Chinese porcelain.

Peter the Great's House

The neighbouring palace reserved for the Estonian head of state (closed to the public) stands near the modest four-room house of Peter the Great built in 1714 pending completion of the Kadriorg Summer Palace. Now a museum *(Peeteri Majamuuseum)*, the house was restored by Tsar Alexander I who provided it with the furniture of both Peter and Catherine the Great, two-thirds of it miraculously surviving to the present day.

Pirita

Beyond Kadriorg Park, a long promenade *(Pirita Tee)* follows the Bay of Tallinn to the beach of Pirita and its yachting harbour. It was here that the yachting regatta of Moscow's Olympic Games was held in 1980. One of its attractions is an old Estonian submarine, the *Lembit*, built in a British shipyard in 1936.

Just the other side of the river is the proud silhouette of the gabled Convent and Monastery of St Bridget *(Pirita Klooster)*. Founded in 1407, it was in large part destroyed in the siege of Ivan the Terrible in 1577. The nuns occupied the northern half and the monks the southern half.

Rocca al Mare

About 10 km west of Tallinn on the shore of the Gulf of Kopli, the Rocca al Mare open-air museum presents an ensemble of 70 rustic buildings at the heart of a vast forest. They display Estonian daily life from the 17th to the early 20th centuries. Along the paths you will come across the pretty wooden chapel of Sutlepa (17th century), one of the last in the country,

18th-century windmills, an old-fashioned school, complete with classroom benches, inkwells and blackboard. Visits are conducted by costumed tour-guides while others stage folklore pageants.

Beaches

The people of Tallinn enjoy the many beaches on the Gulf of Finland west of town. They include Vääna-Jõesuu, Kloogaranna and Lohusalu. Thanks to the Soviet period, they were saved from property developers. Rather than large-scale beach resorts, they offer small harbours, vast pine groves accessible along rambling paths and strips of warm sand welcoming picnickers.

Old wooden mill at the open-air museum of Rocca al Mare.

East of Tallinn, the coast is indented by deep bays with a backdrop of pinewoods, beaches and, beyond Laheema, the low cliffs of the Estonian plateau. Sheltered from high seas and tides, relatively shallow, the eastern end of the Gulf of Finland, dying out at the approaches to St Petersburg, seems more like a lake, tranquil in summer, its banks underlined by sand or reeds.

Laheema National Park

Renowned for its fauna (bear, lynx, elk) and its flora (834 classified varieties), Laheema National Park, the largest in present-day Estonia and the oldest in the ex-Soviet Union, covers an area of 680 sq km. Scattered through its forests are peaceful villages and tiny hamlets—most with wooden houses—fields and meadows heavily laden with the scent of hay in summer. And then there are the lakes, the salmon streams and a large expanse of sea. Here three bays separated by long, broad peninsulas, reach deep into the interior.

Käsmu

The smallest of the park's bays, surrounded by forest, is also the most popular, especially around the beach of Võsu, a little resort with houses hidden among the pine trees. An ideal refuge for the fleet in winter, the well-sheltered bay saw its maritime activities develop from the Middle Ages. On the western shore, the town of Käsmu became an important naval shipyard from the 1800s. In 1884 a highly regarded naval college was founded there, attracting many of its students from local families. The village has a pretty Maritime Museum: bottles, model ships, glass floats, old maps assembled by a private collector are strewn around to create a seaman's world full of charm. Nearby, a pretty little white wooden church, Käsmu Kabel, stands between tall trees at the heart of flower-filled cemetery. The peninsula is dotted with rocks left there by the retreating ice; a path, 4 km long, runs all around it.

Vainupea

To the east, all along the Vergi peninsula to Vainupea, granite rocks are scattered the length of the coast. Lighthouses and pocket-size harbours, beaches with a backdrop of pine trees, thatch-roofed houses and the restored huts of Altja fishermen depict an Estonia of yesteryear.

Depending on the season, you'll see ducks, swans, gulls, grebes, sandpipers and snipe bobbing around. The barbed wire that swathed the coast in Soviet times is long forgotten and the coast has opened up to tourism.

Manors

In the interior, the manors of German families who controlled a large part of the country until their expropriation at the end of World War I have mostly been restored. For two centuries the property of the Von der Pahlens, the Baroque-style Palmse Manor (1785) recalls a certain elegant atmosphere of the 18th and 19th centuries. The manor houses in its various annexes a museum of vintage cars and motor bicycles, as well as the national park's main information centre. Other manors can be visited at Vihula, Sagadi (a neoclassical residence housing a forestry museum) and Kolga. Further east, the ruins of the Toolse Castle (1471) reveal traces of its builders, the Knights of the Livonian Order.

The Northeast

Beyond Lahemaa Park, northeast Estonia attracts few visitors to its more built-up industrialized region, inhabited mostly by Russians who emigrated in Soviet days. In the town, the hammer and sickle symbols and portraits of Lenin and Marx have not altogether disappeared. Once a cause for alarm, the pollution resulting from the oil industry and phosphorus mining has been greatly reduced since independence.

The Coast

With time in hand, you can make a pleasant tour along the wild, unspoiled coast. See the fortified 16th-century Purtse Manor with its whitewashed walls and orange roof-tiles, then the low limestone cliffs of the Estonian plateau plummeting into the Baltic in a tangle of forest. The coast road running along the top of the escarpment commands a pretty view over the Gulf of Finland. At the western entrance to the hamlet of Valaste, a stairway hugging the cliffside looks across to Estonia's highest waterfall (25 m).

Narva

Closer to St Petersburg than to Tallinn, the large town of Narva, 90 percent Russian-speaking, sits on the river of the same name, marking the frontier with Russia. Largely destroyed in World War II, it has held on to a formidable Danish castle, the 13th-century Fort Narva. An annex houses a history museum. Opposite, rising above the blue waters of the Narva, are the walls and pepper-pot corner-towers of the Russian fortress of Ivangorod.

Lake Peïpous

The Narva, which flows into the Gulf of Finland opposite the old Soviet beach resort of Narva-Jõe-suu, starts out from the reservoir formed by Lake Peïpous (*Peipsi järv*). Covering 3555 sq km, it constitutes almost the entire frontier separating Estonia from Russia. Frozen over each winter, it is bordered to the northwest by sand dunes and beaches which many rightly consider the finest in the country. The tradition-minded region attracts few visitors. It is the domain of the Russian-speaking Old Believers.

Pühtitsa

Between Kohtla-Järve and the lake, the village of Kuremäe has grown up around the great Russian Orthodox convent of Pühtitsa (*Kuremäe Klooster*), founded at the end of the 19th century. Superb with its green onion-bulb domes, rose garden and neatly arranged piles of logs for firewood, the place has a timeless but very lively character, and is still inhabited by its nuns and novices.

Beaches

Lake Peïpous hides away its finest beaches along the northwest shore: in particular at Kauksi, an ideal setting for bathing or a picnic beneath the pine trees, or at Uusküla, a village with gaily painted wooden houses. Further south, the *isba* log-houses of Raja extend along the lakeshore dominated now by beds of reeds and fish-vendors. It also has a wooden Russian Orthodox chapel.

Tartu

Since the 6th century, a hilltop Estonian bastion has commanded the right bank of the River Emajõgi. Founded with the name of Yuryev in 1030 by Prince Yaroslav the Great of Kiev, the town grew under the control of the Teutonic Knights (who in 1224 renamed it Dorpat, a name it bore until 1920) and joined the Hanseatic League. Since the foundation of its university by Gustavus Adolphus of Sweden in 1632, Tartu has been the country's main centre of learning. It was here that the movement for a national renaissance was born in the 19th century. Over the years, the country's second-largest city (population now 115,000) suffered considerably from wars and fires.

Town Hall Square

Covered with paving stones, Raekoja plats provides the focus of the city centre. On the west side, the rose-coloured edifice of the Town Hall (1789), crowned by a belfry, overlooks an attractive Lovers' Fountain, sculpted by Estonian artist Marti Karmen in 1999.

The square's neoclassical buildings date from the late 18th century, part of Tartu's reconstruction following the great fire of 1775. The finest are at No.8, No.16, former residence of the Princess of Courland, No.18 with its *trompe l'oeil* windows (now the Kivisilla Art Gallery) and No.20 (late 19th century). Behind the Town Hall, the Baroque building at No. 2 is the only one to have escaped the fire.

Tartu University

From the square, you can see the monumental university building (*Ülikool*) whose porticoed southern façade has become the emblem of higher learning in Estonia. Inaugurated in 1809, it now houses a museum of local art, but also boasting one of the two death masks of philosopher Immanuel Kant, whose home was in nearby Koenigsberg (Kaliningrad).

St John's Church

To the north of the square is the sturdy square tower of St John's Church (*Jaani Kirik*) founded in 1330. Badly damaged in World War II, it is once more open to the public though restoration is continuing on many of its celebrated terracotta figures. The neighbouring house at Jaani Street 16 is home to the municipal museum of 19th-century Tartu (*Linnakodaniku Muuseum*).

Cathedral

West of Raekoja plats up on Cathedral Hill (*Toomemägi*) was the town's original citadel. Today it is the site of a spacious park where strollers can see the eloquent ruins of the great three-aisled Gothic cathedral. No doubt dating back to the late 13th century, it added twin towers in the 15th century, an exceptional feature for the Baltic States. The church was abandoned after the Livonian War (1558–82). In 1806, the choir was rebuilt to house a library and is today a University's History Museum. Higher up the hill are the few surviving remains of the citadel, including a sacrificial altar-stone.

Museums

The outstanding Estonian National Museum (*Eesti Rahva Muuseum*), south of Toomemägi, traces the history of the country and its folklore, while housing a remarkable collection of paintings.

On the other side of River Emajögi, the Town Museum devoted to the city's past is housed in a newly restored neoclassical building at 23 Narva Mantee.

With its winters under heavy snow, wilder and more traditional in style than the rest of the country, the southeast is almost entirely covered by forest. The terrain is also more uneven, though nothing drastic, a series of valleys, wooded hills, the highest just 318 m, and intersected by river and lakes.

Otepää

Some 40 km south of Tartu, the little town of Otepää with its smart wooden houses is one of the Estonians' favourite destinations for celebrating the summer solstice. In the winter it becomes a ski resort. From its long history the town preserves a few sparse traces on Castle Hill (Linnamägi) inhabited since the earliest Christian era. The walk to the top is worthwhile for the grand view over the patchwork of wooded hillocks and flowery meadows.

At the foot of the hill, the 17th-century church is built against another rise. It was here, according to plaques on the façade, that the Estonian national flag was created in 1884—blue for the sky and confidence, black for the earth and painful past, and white for snow and freedom.

Lake Püha

Just south of Otepää, the charming Lake Püha is dotted with small wooded islets and its shores embraced by dense beds of reeds and stretches of forests. A 13-km foot- and cycle-path makes a complete circuit of the lake.

Võru and its Region

Main township in the southeast, Võru gives access to the Haanja Upland encompassing Suur Munamägi, which at 318 m is the highest point in the Baltic States. The wooded hill is crowned by an observation tower with a panoramic view over the region and its forests. A road leads 10 km westwards through the bucolic Nightingale Valley (Ööbikuorg) to the village of Rõuge built at the edge of a chain of seven lakes.

SUMMER SOLSTICE

For Estonians, one day more than all others expresses their national identity: Jaanipäev, the Feast of St John celebrating the summer solstice and the return of fine weather. Drawing on the country's rich pagan roots, it is an opportunity for friends to meet up again around a great joyful bonfire, to drink, sing their heads off and dance the night away.

Enjoy the wonders of nature on the shores of Lake Püha, south of Otepää.

Further on, the area bordering on Latvia sinks into the marshland of Paganamaa, "Devil's Country" and its remote villages.

Setu Country

The tiny pocket of land bordered by Latvia to the south and Lake Pskov to the east is Setu Country *(Setumaa)*, of which the main part is located in Russia. This Finno-Ugric people, close to the Estonians, adopted the Russian Orthodox faith at the time when the region was ruled by the Tsars. A newly awakened consciousness of the Setu identity—hitherto subject to the pressures of Estonian and Russian national-ism—is encouraging the preservation of the local language, but most of its speakers are now quite old. Some of their songs are believed to be 5,000 years old.

At Obinitsa, be sure to visit the fascinating little Setu Heritage Museum *(Seto muuseumitarö)*. Installed in a beautiful little wooden house and log cabins, it preserves major elements of the Setu past: costumes embroidered in warm colours, bridal trousseaus, implements and artefacts.

On the outskirts of the village trees provide shade for a wooden church of 1897. Another museum at Värska is devoted to Setu music, cuisine and farm work. 23

THE HEART OF ESTONIA
Lake Võrts, Soomaa National Park, Viljandi

Lake Võrts

West of Tartu, the country's second biggest lake (266 sq m, but nowhere deeper than 6 m) forms a veritable inland sea surrounded by beds of reeds, with a woodland backdrop. Here and there, houses peep out from beneath the pine trees with farming villages behind them. Footpaths lead to the lakeshore for a day's fishing, a canoe trip, even a little windsurfing, or just to commune with nature for a picnic or a campfire under the stars.

Soomaa National Park

To the northwest, the lake borders on the great Soomaa National Park (371 sq km), created in 1993. The nature reserve shelters a vast area of marshland and mud pools, with forests and meadows flooded in the springtime. Water seeps over a third of the terrain in this overly flat country where the flooding was long considered a season apart. With the exception of a few elevated

pathways, you tour the park in a canoe or *haabja*, a sort of dugout hewn from the trunk of an aspen tree. There's little likelihood of your spotting any of the bear, wolf and lynx present in the area, but should occasionally see elk, beaver or flying squirrel.

Viljandi

Conquered by the Teutonic Knights, Viljandi belonged for a time to the Hanseatic League. Nowadays a quiet little town, it retains a few traces of its heyday, with colourful wooden houses in the centre, and the ruins of the Teutonic castle looming on high.

Built in the middle of parkland, which provides a popular recreation spot for the residents, the town overlooks an elongated lake. At the lower end is the pretty church of St John *(Jaani Kirik)* with its sturdy clock tower. The handsome 18th-century building at No. 10 Kindral Laidoreri Square is also worth a visit; it houses the local museum.

Pärnu

From the first sign of fine weather, holidaymakers head for its beach and its attractions—nightclubs, bars, concerts, festivals, amusement park, nothing is lacking for Pärnu to be considered the country's summer capital and main beach resort (population 51,000). The trading city founded in 1251 by Bishop Henry and enlisted in the Hanseatic League 15 years later became a holiday resort in 19th century, enjoying its golden era from 1890 to 1930. In the Soviet era, its sanatoriums specializing in therapeutic mud baths welcomed meritorious workers from every corner of the Soviet Union. Closed because of pollution at the time of independence, the beach has been cleaned up and sports a European Union blue flag of excellence, and the city centre restored from top to bottom.

City Centre

The heart of town occupies a peninsula formed by the River Pärnu and the Gulf of Livonia. Entrance to town was originally through the Tallinn Gate, which backs on to the large Vallikäär Park. Here you can see the last remains of the 17th-century Swedish fortifications. Further on, in Uus Street, is the neoclassical palace of the old Town Hall (1797), once the residence of wealthy merchant. Nearby is the brightly coloured Russian Orthodox St Catherine's Church (Ekateriina Kirik) built in 1768, with an ornate interior. Take Nikolai Street to the Lutheran Church of Elizabeth (Eliisabeti Kirik), built in 1747 for the Tsarina Elizabeth. To one side, at Kuninga Street 24, is a restored warehouse of 1694.

Pühavaimu Street crosses Rüütli, the main shopping street in the pedestrian district, before coming to some restored dwellings: No.10, a wooden house with a carved and painted door; No.8, the Baroque-style Steinert House (1674) with its storehouse, to which a neoclassical entrance has been added in the form of triumphal arch; and the Heno House (1670) also Baroque with a roof notable for its sculptures of a couple of scowling characters.

The lane squeezing in between the houses at Nos. 8 and 10 leads to what is now a hotel in a fine house of 1658. Turn right around a block of houses to take a look at the so-called Red Tower (Punane Torn), Hommiku Street 11, last vestige of the fortifications built in the 15th century. Today it is white and houses a souvenir shop.

25

Freshly painted houses brighten up the resort of Pärnu.

Pärnu Museum

In a converted granary at 4, Aida Street, the museum traces the story of the town and region from the Stone Age to the 20th century. Exhibitions draw on its considerable ethnographic collections, and there's a room furnished in Soviet style.

Modern Art Museum

This recent museum has already acquired a reputation for originality. The tone is set at the entrance by a decapitated statue of Lenin with a rotating police-car light in place of his head. Recently, summer exhibitions have been devoted to the theme of sexuality in art, notably the photos of Robert Mapplethorpe and the drawings of Jean Cocteau.

Beach

Further south you will find the beach, long, broad and gently sloping down to the sea. While adults enjoy the warm sands, the children take advantage of the games and other attraction set up for them. Behind the beach, the old rose-coloured spa facilities back onto the Ranna Park. At the beach's west end, where the River Pärnu flows in the sea, the long pier built under Catherine the Great makes a popular promenade.

Haapsalu

Equidistant between Pärnu and Tallinn, Haapsalu is a regular stop on the route to the Island of Hiiumaa. This beach and spa resort made its reputation in the 19th century with its therapeutic mud baths, much appreciated by the Russian Imperial family. Aafrikarand, the "African Beach" was a popular haunt of a fellow named Tchaikovsky. If Estonian summer holidaymakers still come here in great number today, it is in part to rediscover the traces of its golden era.

City Centre

The Bishop's Castle (1279), left partly in ruin but still surrounded by ramparts with turrets and bastions, recalls the era when Haapsalu was the episcopal residence following the Lithuanians' destruction of Pärnu. The Teutonic Knights built side by side the castle, in which one wing houses a museum, and the cathedral. This is the largest German-style hall church in the Baltic States (with nave and aisles of the same height). Its construction conforms to the very sober Cistercian order, with Gothic vaulting and capitals carved with Romanesque-style floral motifs. After Peter the Great's troops destroyed its roof during his Northern Wars, the church was used only in the summer months.

Museums

Opposite the castle entrance on Lossi Square, take a quick look at the Läänemaa Museum devoted to local history, and at St John's Church *(Jaani Kirik)* dating back to the 16th and 17th centuries. In addition there's a Railway Museum at the south end of town and, at the other end, the charming little Museum of Estonia's Swedish People *(Raanarootsi Muuseum)*, exploring the history and daily life of the 8,000 Swedes, for the most part fishermen, who lived along the country's west coast until 1944.

ESTONIA'S SWEDES

The Noarootsi jutting out north of Haapsalu, the islands of Vormsi and Hiimuaa, just facing it, and the little isle of Osmusaar further north were inhabited for a long period by the Swedes. Settled there since the 13th century in the wake of the Danish conquests, they preserved for centuries their medieval language and customs. At the end of World War II, fearing the arrival of the Soviets, many left for a mother country they had never seen. Today, the survivors and their children come back to visit the traces of their past.

Lying between the Baltic Sea and the Gulf of Livonia, the Estonian islands form to the west a natural barrier, a swarm of hundreds of islands and islets, of which the smallest, just clumps of stony earth, scarcely stick out above the water. With its low salt-content and no tides, the water is smothered in vegetation, less sea than swamp.

On land, the little roads are bordered by bucolic farm country, a mixture of fields blooming in season with cornflowers and poppies and broad forests, villages and old windmills.

Hiiumaa

From Rohuküla, 10 km from Haapsalu, the ferry makes several crossings per day to the Hiiumaa Island, Estonia's second-biggest (1,023 sq km).

The boat arrives on the east coast near the little town of Suuremõisa. Here you will find the best-preserved manors of the old German landed aristocracy; they were built in late-Baroque style from 1755 to 1760.

Nearby, the church of Pühalepa (1257), the island's oldest, is surrounded by a little overgrown cemetery. In olden days, women were allowed in only by the little side-door.

Kärdla

Further west, Kärdla is the island's main town. In fact it's a simple little place with its houses, many of them built of wood, half-hidden among the trees. Visit the little Hiiumaa Museum, with an emphasis mainly on the 19th century when Kärdla had a clothing factory.

Tahkuna Peninsula

The peninsula was inhabited from 1400 by Swedes, whom the Russian authorities forced to emigrate to the Ukraine in 1781. Of the 1,200 who left, less than half reached their destination nine months later. They celebrated their last Mass at Ristimägi, the Hill of the Crosses, along the road to Kõgessaare. It became the custom for passers-by to fashion a makeshift cross with branches or stones as a prayer for their return. They are simply laid out on the ground or planted there, in their hundreds. In 1929, the Ukrainian Swedes' descendants were authorized to "return" to Sweden; rather than stay in a place that had never been their home, some of them emigrated to Canada, some returned to Ukraine.

Not far from the village of Malvaste, in a clearing north of Hiiumaa Island is a group of

Low thatched barns in the north of Hiiumaa island.

farmhouses *(mihkli)*, barns and old-fashioned saunas, all built with log-walls and thatched roofs. The end of the peninsula is guarded by an old lighthouse manufactured in France and a monument erected in memory of the ferry victims of the *Estonia* shipwreck. It is the custom to ring the bell in their memory.

Kõpu Lighthouse

West of Hiiumaa is another peninsula, longer and narrower. Plumb in the middle, a lighthouse stands proudly since 1531—third-oldest in the world to have never stopped working. A quite astonishing sight with its great buttresses and somehow quirky spiral staircase, its top, 37 m up, offers a grand panoramic view of the surrounding forest.

Kaïna and Kassari

On the east side of the island, most of the tourist facilities are grouped around the big village of Kaïna. The nearby bay of the same name, almost shut off at both ends, bordered on the south by the tip of Kassari Island, looks more like a great pond than a bay. The lush vegetation of its shores attracts a large number of migratory birds, which has led to the establishment here of a bird sanctuary.

29

On Kassari, two sites are worth a visit: the Hiiumaa History Museum *(Hiiumaa Koduloomuuseum)* and the delightful thatch-roofed chapel *(Kassari Kabel)*, last one of its kind in Estonia. It was built in the 18th century to save the islanders the trouble of having to cross the marshes to attend Mass in Pühalepa.

At the south end, the narrow Sääretirp peninsula is an ideal place for a picnic.

Saaremaa

The largest island in Estonia (2673 sq km), indeed in the whole Baltic Sea, has a very rustic look—windmills, peaceful villages, and a few thatch-roofed cottages.

Conquered and reconquered scores of times, Saaremaa was German for three centuries, then in turn Danish, Swedish and Russian. During World War II, the majority of its Swedish population chose exile. Of its 56,000 inhabitants in 1939, it numbered only 38,000 in 1945, a figure that has remained roughly the same ever since.

In summer, from Sõru south of Hiiumaa, a ferry makes three trips a day to Saaremaa. But most people come from Virtsu on the mainland, via Muhu. Together, Saaremaa and Muhu form one rural district and are linked by a causeway.

Kuressaare

The main town of the Saaremaa district, Kuressaare nestles in the heart of a narrow bay on the island's south coast. Formerly a Soviet tourist resort, it has found a new lease of life as an important spa centre boasting several big sanatoriums.

On Kesk väljak Square, the handsome Baroque Town Hall (1670) is guarded by two old stone lions. Opposite, the Weighing House *(Vaekoda)* built in 1633 is now a pub.

Episcopal Castle

Further south, overlooking the last reaches of the Bay of Kuressaare, the Episcopal Castle stands guard, unperturbed since it was first erected between 1340 and 1380 as a dependency of Haapsalu diocese. Built in late-Gothic style on its own islet, it is still protected by its 15th-century fortifications with 7-m walls, earthworks, and large moats added by the Danes 200 years later. The castle proper, which was also a prison, opens onto a square inner courtyard framed by corner bastions. In all the Baltic States, it is the one castle to have survived the vagaries of history with so few changes. It houses the regional museum divided into two sections. The larger part is devoted to the island's historical development, the other to its natural history. Notice in particular the castle's handsome refectory with its cross vaulted ceiling.

Around the Island

A trip to the west of the island takes you along the narrow finger of the Sõrve peninsula, isolated and remote, and to the Viidumäe botanical nature reserve where they have identified 700 varieties of plants and 630 different kinds of butterfly.

At Viki, near Kihelkonna, an old farm from the 1850s and its annexes (barn, mill and granary) have been transformed into an open-air museum *(Mihkli Talumuuseum)*.

Just to the west, Vilsandi National Park covers the island of the same name and 160 other islets in the Baltic, attracting thousands of migratory birds.

A meteorite which fell 5,000 to 7,000 years ago at Kaali in the centre of Kuressaare left a crater 110 m wide *(Meteoriidikrater)*, today filled by a little lake. Further on, the five windmills of Angla line the road in a long-used windblown spot. One of them, beautifully restored, has preserved its mechanism.

The fortified church of Karja, 2 km away, is well worth a sidetrip. Built like so many others by the Teutonic Knights at the end of the 13th century, it has a wealth of exceptional architectural detail

from the late-Romanesque era: sculpted capitals on the porch and in the nave, paintings in the choir representing striking mystical symbols and a magnificent bas-relief of the Crucifixion incorporated in the outer right wall.

All the way east, other sites recall the Germanic past, including the superb church of Pöide, 13th-century centre of the Order of the Sword Brethren, and the ruins of their castle at Orissaare, destroyed by a peasant uprising in 1343.

Muhu

Joined by a causeway to Saaremaa and by a frequently travelling ferry from Virtsu on the mainland, the smaller island of Muhu (206 sq km) is nonetheless Estonia's third largest. The windmill museum of Eemu *(Eemu Tuulik)*, built in 1881, is once more in working order. Opposite, a small road leads to the village-museum of Koguva *(Kugula Küla Mumu Muuseum)*. Its thatch-roofed houses, some of them still inhabited, and its school-museum date back to the 19th century. The exhibition displays the island's traditions, in particular those concerning its costumes. Further on, the German church of Liiva *(Muhu Katarina Kirik)* built in the 13th and 14th centuries is known for its nautical frescoes. 31

Dining Out

Estonian cuisine is a blend of multiple influences, in particular German and Russian, and expresses a preference for heartiness and simplicity. In the cities, most restaurants offer a bilingual menu. You also have a choice of the many *kohvik* (cafés) and pastry-shops.

Before sitting down to eat, Estonians often like to get together for a beer helped down by a selection of appetizers—pieces of fried chicken, for instance, or fried or boiled meatballs dipped in sour cream.

When it comes down to the main meal, you may expect marinated fish for starters, in particular mackerel and herring, the latter very tender, served with beetroot *(rossolye)* or onions and potatoes and again with sour cream. Soups are also popular—sauerkraut *(hapukapsa)*, salmon *(lõhesupp)*, meat, mushrooms Russian-style *(seljanka)*, beetroot borsch, but they may need spicing up. Another speciality is cold veal in aspic *(sült)*.

Salads *(salatid)* are not always a suitable choice for vegetarians since most of them are composed of more meat—smoked ham, sausage or salami—than green vegetables.

Though they do eat a lot of fish, especially salmon *(lõhe)*, Estonians have a distinct preference for meat—generally cooked medium whatever the kind. Pork may be served with sauerkraut *(seapraad hapukapsaga)*,cut into escalopes with mushrooms, onions or potato pancakes, marinated in herbs *(seafille ürdin-marinaadis)* or stewed *(ahjuliha)*, like beef. Steaks are often prepared with tomatoes and garlic, as is chicken, which may also come smoked *(suitsukanapada)*. Wild boar is popular among game in season. For sound ecological reasons, we recommend you to avoid bear meat if it is offered. The p in Estonian is pronounced like a b, so *spaghetti bolognese* will appear on the menu as *polognese*.

For dessert, the choices may be limited to an Estonian semolina pudding *(mannakreem piimaga)*, pancakes with wild-berry jam, fruit salads and ice creams.

Drinks

Estonians have taken to beer (Saku and A. le Coq). They also like shots of aquavit, Estonian or Russian vodka, as well as sweet liqueurs of cherry, strawberry or cranberry.

Shopping

above all very attractive Jacquard sweaters in Scandinavian geometric snowflake patterns, generally at prices two or three times cheaper than in the other northern European countries.

Leather goods are another Estonian speciality—bags, book-jackets, etc. As for ceramics, while the beer mugs and tea or coffee services may be quite attractive, some decorative pieces are undeniably kitsch.

Jewellery is reasonably priced, mostly in silver and especially amber, as in the other Baltic States from which the fossilized resin is imported.

Many visitors also like to take away a bottle of Estonian vodka (from Saaremaa), fruit liqueurs or Vana Tallinn, a liqueur created after World War II reminiscent of rum but rather bitter—very good with coffee. Cranberry liqueur will certainly intrigue your guests back home.

In Tallinn, the Lower Town is the best place to do your shopping, especially the pretty St Catherine's Passage (*Katariina käik*).

When it comes to *suveniird*, Estonian draws on its own raw materials and traditional know-how. Wood is fashioned by seasoned craftsmen into all sorts of appealing toys (cars, dolls, farm animals) and rustic kitchen utensils such as tablemats, chopping boards, wooden spoons, kitchen forks, salad servers in juniper wood and birch wood latticework baskets. More ornate, delicately carved wooden flowers are highly appreciated. Wickerwork is used for trays, shopping-baskets or picnic hampers.

Among the textile goods, you will find beautiful traditional embroidered fabrics and wall hangings in heavy or finely woven linen, along with napkins and table sets. The knitwear includes fancy socks, bonnets, gloves and

The Hard Facts

Airport
Located 4 km from the city centre, the recently renovated Tallinn Airport is easily reached by the No. 2 bus or minibus. If you take a taxi, make sure the meter is working before you set off.

Climate
The best time to visit Estonia is in summer, from early June to the end of August. Autumn arrives early, winter is long with heavy snows and the spring can transform the land into a veritable quagmire.

Currency
Until Estonia adopts the Euro (now planned for January 1, 2010), the unit of currency is the Estonian *Kroon* or crown (*EEK or kr.*) divided into 100 *senti,* with coins from 5 to 50 *senti,* 1 to 5 crowns, and banknotes from 1 to 500 crowns.

Apart from the many currency exchange offices, cash distributor machines (ATMs) are available in most towns. Credit cards are widely accepted in the cities but less so away from the main tourist areas.

Electricity
220 Volts, 50 Hz.

Opening Hours
Shops generally open Monday to Friday 10 a.m.–6 p.m., Saturday to 3 or 5 p.m. Shopping malls close at 9 to 11p.m. Museums are nearly all closed on Monday, sometimes also on Tuesday.

Telephone
Cabins operate with phone cards sold in newspaper kiosks and the post office. As elsewhere in the European Union, the international prefix is 00 followed by the country code and your correspondent's number.

Time
Standard time is GMT+2 from November to March and GMT+3 from April to October. When it is noon in London, it is 2pm in Tallinn.

Tipping
Practically unknown a few years ago, tipping is become more and more the custom (up to 10%).

Toilets
Women's toilets have a triangle pointing up (like a skirt) or the letter N on the door. Men's toilets have an inverted triangle (like a broad-shouldered man) or an M on the door.

LATVIA

This Way Latvia

Latvian Renaissance

Bolstered by the burgeoning commercial and industrial prosperity of Riga, its capital, and the rural charms of its hinterland, Latvia is enjoying the fruits of its hard-won national unity. Sandwiched between Estonia to the north and Lithuania to the south, Latvia has a land area of 64,589 sq km. The landscape is by and large flat, alternating forests and fields. The fine weather brings out poppies, cornflowers, and a sea of blue lupins, and storks set to building their nests. It is also dotted with thousands of lakes and rivers, of which the two biggest have left their historical mark— the Daugava, on whose banks Riga was founded, and the Gauja, in whose valley you will see the ruins of medieval castles. To the west, Latvia is marked by the deep curve of the Gulf of Riga.

Five tribes have settled the country, giving their name to each of its regions, Couronians to the west *(Kurzeme)*, Semigallians in the centre and south *(Zemgale)*, Letts or Latgallians north of the Daugava *(Latgale)*, where the ethnic Latvians evolved separately to give their name to the whole country, and the Selonians to the southeast *(Selija)*. The non-Baltic Livs, closely related to the Estonians, inhabited the Livonian coastal region *(Vidzeme)* on the Gulf of Riga and long preserved their Finno-Ugric language.

The ethnic groups gradually disappeared to merge into one Latvian people. Fierce defenders of their independence, close to their peasant and "pagan" roots, the Latvians were converted to Christianity only by armed force from the 13th century. Catholic in the southeast, which was for long under Polish rule, Lutheran Protestant everywhere else, they remain fervent observers of the millennial traditions of the summer solstice.

Since independence, national pride is soothing the wounds of a painful history and the future is looking brighter. The Latvian language, threatened for a while by Russification, has found its way back into the school curriculum. It's true that Latvians are only a small majority in their own country (58%). Russian-speaking immigrants, brought in by the Soviet Union to promote industrial development and strengthen the armed forces, still represent about a third of the 2.3 million population. Intercourse between the communities is not very active.

Flashback

2500 BC	The territory of Latvia is settled by Indo-European tribes and by the Livs, a Finno-Ugric people related linguistically to the Estonians and Finns.
12th century AD	German merchants create links with tribes living along the River Daugava. Near the estuary, a trading post is established at Riga in 1158. The first missionaries follow soon after but have little success with the pagan Balts.
13th–15th centuries	Riga's foundation as a town takes place in 1201 under the auspices of Bishop Albrecht. At the urging of Pope Innocent III, a crusade is launched to break resistance to proselytism among the Livs. Created for the purpose, the Order of the Sword Brethren spreads terror through the region (formally named Livonia, including southern part of present-day Estonia). In 1207, a semblance of peace is restored and power over the territory is shared between the Bishop of Riga and the knights of the Order. The Sword Brethren form the Livonian Order, easternmost outpost of the Teutonic Knights. By 1290, eight years after Riga joins the Hanseatic League, all resistance by the Balts is eliminated. Over the next two centuries, rivalries among the all-powerful Livonian Order, the archbishop and the city fathers of Riga plunged the territory into internecine battles.
16th–19th centuries	The 16th century, which sees the elimination of Germanic power, is one of constant conflicts: those linked with the Reformation (1522), then with the territorial appetites of Livonia's neighbours. In 1561, the last Master of the Order, having retreated to the duchy of Courland, accepts the suzerainty of the great Polish-Lithuanian kingdom over the rest of the country. This in turn, with the exception of the southeast, falls to the Swedes following their war with Poland. In 1621, they are welcomed with relief by the Protestants of Riga. Less than a century later, Livonia is conquered by Tsar Peter the Great during the Great Northern War of 1700. Courland is annexed to Russia after the third carve-up of Poland in 1795. The two provinces remain to all intents and purposes in the hands of the "Baltic Barons", heirs of the Germanic Knights. Russia

imposes its feudal law until 1819. In the 19th century, Riga becomes the third industrial city of the Russian Empire. It experiences a dazzling national reawakening, marked by the creation in 1873 of a landmark festival of Latvian folksongs.

20th century–present

The country is highly active in the first Russian Revolution of 1905. After its occupation by German troops in World War I, Latvia declares itself independent and joins the League of Nations in 1921. Parliamentary democracy gives way in 1934 to the repressive authoritarian (but economically prosperous) government of Karlis Ulmanis, succeeded by Soviet occupation of Latvia in 1940. Thousands of Latvians are executed or deported to Siberia. The German Army invades Latvia in the summer of 1941; 90 per cent of the country's 70,000 Jews are murdered by the Germans and their Latvian collaborators. Recaptured by the Red Army in 1944, the country is subjected to a new wave of deportations. Resistance continues in the forests until 1956. Meanwhile, many Russians are relocated to Latvia to further develop its industrialization. From 1988, encouraged by Mikhail Gorbachev's reformist policies, the Latvians demonstrate in the streets of Riga against the rule of the Soviet Union; a new Popular Front wins a majority in the parliamentary elections of 1990. After a referendum, Latvia restores its independence in 1991. The country joins NATO in 2004 and enters the European Union.

On the Scene

The charming historic quarters of Riga have been declared a UNESCO World Heritage Site since 1997. In the modern neighbourhoods, it is the splendid Art Nouveau buildings that attract the visitors' attention.

Outside the capital, Latvia's four provinces have many cultural curiosities to offer in a variety of landscapes: Vidzeme and the Gauja Valley with its forts and castles; Latgale, "country of the blue lakes"; historic Zemgale at the heart of Latvia with its Baroque palace of Rundāle; and Kurzeme in the country's west and northwest, facing the sea.

▶ RIGA

Old Town (north), Old Town (south),
New Town, Outside the City

Almost a third of the national population live in Riga, the Baltic States' biggest town and main industrial centre. Many Russian soldiers have chosen to take their retirement here; indeed more than 40 per cent of the 760,000 inhabitants are not Latvian. With its historic centre restored for the town's 800th anniversary in 2001, the Latvian capital can proudly claim to be one of the most beautiful medieval cities in Northern Europe. And it manages to combine this traditional charm with considerable modern style and dynamism.

During the first millennium of the Christian era, tribes of Livs and Balts made their way to trade downstream on the River Daugava. Focussing on this great regional market centre, Germanic conquerors founded Riga as a trading post in 1201 as part of a Christian crusade to convert the "pagans". The place was colonized by craftsmen, merchants, churchmen and sundry adventurers from Bremen and the rest of northern Germany. From 1207, the budding city built its first ramparts. Riga became a Hanseatic port in 1282, the stronghold of the

Livonian Knights for over three centuries. It enjoyed a brilliant heyday in the Middle Ages, to which some remarkable buildings still testify. From the 16th century, a procession of invaders began—Poles, Swedes, Russians, each leaving a trace of their passage. More recently, exploiting the town's strategic location, especially the port that remained ice-free for most of the winter, the Soviets anchored their mighty Baltic fleet there.

Old Town (North)

On the right bank of the Daugava, the historic centre (Vecrīga) is separated from the New Town to the east by a crescent of parks. Largely closed to traffic, it owes its appeal to cobblestoned streets and lanes lined with 17th- and 18th-century houses, Germanic warehouses and Gothic churches, in all, 79 buildings classified as historic monuments. In summer, a 60-minute river cruise offers a leisurely way to get an overall view.

Dom Cathedral

Focus of the northern half of Old Town is the majestic Dom Cathedral (Doma Baznīca), the biggest in the Baltic States. Built in late-Romanesque style in 1211 under Bishop Albrecht, the church, now Protestant, was modified several times over the centuries but without abandoning its sturdy brick walls, 2 m thick. The dome of the belltower is crowned by a slender spire on which stands a gilded cock. The Baroque tower (90 m) replaced a much taller (140 m) but more rickety one in 1776. Inside the church, Reformation iconoclasts—followed later by a big fire in 1547—destroyed statues of the saints and other treasures; the interior, largely 17th-century, is notable now for its splendid stained-glass windows and a huge organ built in 1884, boasting 6,768 pipes. Their stunning sonority can be heard in year-round concerts.

Cathedral Gallery

The gallery (Doma krusteja), where medieval processions led from the Cathedral to its cloister, is a veritable masterpiece of Baltic Romanesque (early 13th century). Covered on three sides by vaulted roofs, the gallery shelters a museum with a remarkable collection of cannons, wooden gun carriages, fragments of architecture and wrought iron work, and stained-glass. Be sure to see the so-called Head of Salaspils, a monumental stone idol weighing 780 kilos, of uncertain date, excavated in the year 2000. The cathedral's original cockerel weathervane, 2 m high, is also on display after long years of faithful service from 1595 to 1985.

RIGA'S GOLDEN LEGEND

Once upon a time, an exceptionally tall, strong man answering to the name of Kristops carried travellers across the River Daugava on his back. One day, he found a child all alone on the riverbank. He took him home to his humble dwelling. Next day, when Kristops awoke, the child was no longer there, but in his place was a heap of gold—a fortune used to build the town of Riga.

Museum of History and Navigation

Nearby at Palasta Street 4, the old cloister today houses the Museum of Riga's History and Navigation (Rīgas vēstures un kugniecības muzejs). One section is devoted to this Hanseatic portcity's maritime past, notably with some fine ship models. Another larger department traces the history of the city from its origins to the present day via hundreds of objects of daily life—including furnishings, costumes, photos and paintings—but also the Riga moped manufactured in 1989. Up on the second floor is a 2.36 m tall wooden statue of Big Kristops, Riga's traditional protector against flooding. Dating back to the early 16th century when it stood on the Daugava riverbank, this is one of three such statues—another was posted at the entrance to the city.

Riga Castle

Pils Street leads from Cathedral Square northwest to Riga Castle (Rīga Pils). The residence of the Livonian Knights was built between 1330 and 1353 over what had originally been the Hospital of the Holy Ghost. Destroyed in 1484, it was soon rebuilt, then expanded in the 16th century. Today the buildings house the official residence of the President as well as the Museum of Foreign Art (Arzemju mākslas muzejs) with its diversified collections covering the history of mankind. The most important sections are devoted to the sculpture and painting of western Europe—in particular the Flemish paintings, notably a fine triptych of the Virgin Mary and Child by Jakob van Utrecht. The castle also houses the Rainis Museum of Literature and the History of Latvian Art and the National History Museum (Latvijas vēstures muzejs)—Latvia from the Stone Age to the 19th century, with an interesting folklore section.

Mazā Pils Street

From Castle Square (Pils Laukums), the pretty cobblestoned Mazā Pils Street goes off to the east. The remarkable group of houses at Nos. 17, 19 and 21 are known as the Three Brothers *(Tris brali)*. Once a bakery, the White Brother at No.17, with its gabled roof and Gothic niches, is Riga's oldest dwelling (late 15th century). In the middle, the Baroque Yellow Brother (1646) is home to the Museum of Latvian Architecture, with some interesting maps and building models, while the Green Brother next door is late 17th century.

St James's Church

A lane opposite the Three Brothers leads to St James's Church *(Svētā Jēkaba baznīca)*, a red-brick building founded outside the city walls in 1225. Modified between the 13th and 16th centuries, it has kept the town's lone Gothic spire. Following the expulsion of the Dominicans during the Reformation, it passed into private hands and was used first as a stable and then as a gunsmith's workshop. According to legend, whenever an unfaithful wife passes by the church, its bell, forged in 1480, begins to chime.

Fortifications

Walk past the monumental national Parliament *(Saeima)* built in 1867, near St James's Church, and turn left on Jēkaba Street, then right on Toŗņa Street. Here, the Swedish Gate *(Zviedru vārti)* was built into the city walls during the occupation of 1698 to help the flow of traffic in and out of the Old Town and is now the only surviving gate in the fortifications. Guarded by old cannons set into the rampart, it is topped by an attractive house, the residence of the town executioner. On execution days, it was the custom for him to display a rose in his window.

At the end of the street, which is lined with a handsome collection of well-restored old houses, you can see the tower of the town's gunpowder store *(Pulvertornis)*, the only surviving tower of those built into the walls in the 18th century. It marked the main entrance to the town. To protect its ammunition stores, it was built with walls 2.50 m thick, clearly a good idea when you see the nine Russian cannonballs still lodged there. Today it houses the War Museum devoted to the conflicts of the 20th century.

Cats' House

Coming back to the Cathedral by Meistaru Street, you pass by the famous Cat's House (No.19), an apartment and office building with the figures of two cats perched on its turrets. It's not known why the owner put them up there, but they proved unlucky —he fell to his death while doing it. A second story claims that a 43 later resident, a merchant by trade, turned the cats around so that their backsides faced the house of the Great Guild, which had refused him membership.

Great and Small Guilds

Facing each other at Amatu Street 5 and 6, the Gothic houses of the Great Guild (*Lielā Gilde*) and Small Guild (*Mazā Gilde*) recall the town's mercantile past in the era of the Hanseatic League. At first the Great Guild admitted only Germanic merchants, later adding lawyers, goldsmiths and other prestigious trades. The Small Guild was essentially composed of craftsmen's corporations. The two buildings were extensively restored in the 19th century, losing much of their old patina. But the Great Guild, now a concert hall for the Riga Philharmonic Orchestra, has kept its Münster Hall (1330), originally the merchants' assembly hall, and the Bridal Chamber (1521).

Old Town (south)

Riga's first great buildings, dating from the 13th century, are to be found south of Kaļķu Street, which runs through the middle of the Old Town.

Decorative Arts Museum

The Sword Brethren once worshipped at St George's Church, Skarņu Street 10–16, which now

houses a museum (*Dekoratīvās mākslas muzejs*). This magnificent space with its ancient beams and Romanesque stonework is devoted to fabrics, ceramics and glassware from the late 19th century to the 1960s.

St John's Church

Further down the street, St John's Church (*Jāņa baznīca*), beginning as a simple chapel, became part of Bishop Albrecht's palace. In 1234, his successor Nikolaus presented it as a gift to the Dominicans who turned it into a monastery. After the Reformation the church was rented to the town mayor who for a time used it has a stable for his cattle. Despite its frequent modification, you can still admire its superb rib-vaulted ceiling, choir stalls engraved with the emblem of the Black Heads Fraternity and the series of scenes from the Passion of Christ decorating the balcony that supports the 18th-century organ.

St Peter's Church

Just opposite, the great Lutheran Church of St Peter *(Pētera Baznīca)*, dedicated to the patron saint of Riga, was consecrated at the beginning of the 13th century. The present building, however, a fine example of Gothic architecture, was largely reconstructed in the 15th century. It is used now only for temporary exhibitions. Its western façade has three splendid late 17th-century Baroque portals. It has always been famous for its lofty spire (123 m), originally of wood and frequently destroyed, now (since 1967) of metal. An observation platform in the tower at 72 m (accessible by elevator) offers a striking view over the Old Town's roofs and the River Daugava. Five times a day, the folksong *Riga dimd* ("Riga resounds") is broadcast from the top of the church.

Mārstaļu Street

Extending Skārņu Street to the south, the long Mārstaļu Street was one of the most prestigious addresses in town during the Baroque era. At No. 2, be sure to see the house of a wealthy German merchant Johannes Reitern *(Reiterna Nams,* 1685), today the seat of the Journalists' Associa-

Painted stucco, detail on the House of the Black Heads.

45

tion. Behind No. 8, the interesting little Latvian Photography Museum (*Latvijas fotogrāfijas muzejs*) exhibits old photos, daguerreotypes and historic models of the famous miniature Minox camera originally manufactured (before World War II) in Riga. The museum occupies one of the neighbourhood's many medieval warehouses, with their characteristic hoisting beam jutting out from the upper façade. Most of them are to be found on Alksnaja and Vecplsētas Streets.

Mentzendorff House
Go back up Kungu Street to the corner house at Grēcinieku Street 18. The Mentzendorff House (*Mencendorfa Nams*) is the home of the Riga Citizens Museum

(*Rīdzinieku Mājā muzejs*). The interior, with its period furnishings and paintings, recalls the lifestyle of the wealthy merchant Jürgen Helm who made it his residence in 1695 when he headed the municipal council and was dean of the Small Guild. Notice on the ground floor the warehouse table with its carefully carpentered edges to prevent the thaler coins from falling off. Upstairs, two rooms have frescoes from the early 18th century, one of them a particularly fine group inspired by the paintings of Watteau.

Occupation Museum
To give it its full name, the Museum of the Occupation of Latvia (*Latvijas okupācijas muzejs*) up on Strelnieku Laukums presents one of most compelling—and most controversial—exhibitions in the city. Devoted to the occupation of the country by German and Soviet forces, it was originally known as the Museum of Latvian Red Riflemen, who fought with the Bolsheviks in World War I and whose gigantic monument still towers beside the modern building. The museum now documents the dual post-1940 occupation with photos, memorabilia and personal belongings of prisoners in German concentration camps and Soviet gulags.

WALLED UP ALIVE

In the 15th century, two devout believers eager to demonstrate their faith had themselves walled up alive on the south side of St John's Church, leaving a cross-shaped opening just large enough for people to give them food. The custom was not so rare for the zealots of those days. They died shortly after and were never canonized. The chink in the outer wall can still be seen today.

House of the Black Heads

On Riga's 800th anniversary in 2001, the municipal authorities erected a completely new reconstruction of the famous House of the Black Heads *(Melngalvju Nams)*. The original house of the powerful merchant guild was built in 1344 and destroyed in 1941. The new building respects its original Gothic style with a splendid Flemish Renaissance façade. For many centuries the Black Heads shared their premises with the Great Guild with whom they had close links and frequent squabbles. They separated in 1687. In the basement, a small museum exhibits finds from excavations and various architectural fragments from the original building. Its treasure is a superb *St George Slaying the Dragon* (1622).

New Town

Running along the eastern edge of the Old Town, the canal with its park marks the border of the New Town, which developed in the 19th and early 20th centuries. There among benches and statues is Bastion Hill *(Bastejkalns)*.

Freedom Monument

At the intersection of Brīvības (ex-Lenin) and Raiņa boulevards, Riga's Embassy Row, the Freedom Monument *(Brīvības piemineklis)*, a 1935 sculpture by Kār-

---

> **ZEPPELINS**
>
> Southeast of Old Town is the core of modern Riga with its main railway station and a market once more laden with an abundance of food. The halls date from before World War II, when they served as hangars for a fleet of Zeppelin flying boats.

---

lis Zāle, symbolizes the nation's ardent combat for its independence. The three stars held aloft by Milda, as Latvians have nicknamed this symbol of the state, represent its three historic provinces. The 42-m tall monument somewhat miraculously survived both German and Soviet occupations. To this day, many people place flowers there in memory of victims of the two dictatorships.

Esplanade Park

Brīvības bulivaris runs through Esplanade Park and past the Russian Orthodox Cathedral of Christ's Nativity *(Kristus dzimsanas katedrāle)*. Completed in 1884, it was transformed into a planetarium in the Soviet era but recently returned to Riga's Orthodox community.

On the other side of the park, the national Fine Arts Museum *(Valsts mākslas muzejs)* is housed in a massive, but elegant neoclas-

sical building completed in 1905. Its collections are devoted to Latvian painting from the late 18th century to 1945, with a small section for Russian art.

Close by on the 3rd floor of Skolas Street 6 is the small Jewish Museum tracing the history of Latvia's important Jewish community from the 18th century to the worst moments of World War II, when 90% of the population (then 70,000) was exterminated.

Art Nouveau Buildings

One of Riga's outstanding attractions away from the city centre is the exceptional ensemble of Art Nouveau buildings designed around 1900, among the finest in Europe. Lining the street extending to the north, no one building is like another, thanks to the architects' unbridled imagination and endless innovation. Eizflens Laube, Konstantyns Pēkšēns and Aleksandrs Vanags were considered romantic nationalists, while Mihails Eizenšteins (father of the Soviet Union's most famous film maker, Sergei Eisenstein) was more unabashedly decorative. For their architectural ornament, they all depicted the most improbable fantastical creatures, using bas-reliefs, masks, stucco and sculpture for exotic motifs drawn from ancient mythology and Latvian folklore.

Eizenšteins' work can be seen at Elizabetes Street 10b, designed in 1903 with friezes of white stucco on a blue background. To the right, at Antonija Street 8, notice the dragons guarding the door (1904). On the left, Alberta Street boasts the most ornate designs: the sphinx at No.2a, the dragon and lions at No.4 and at No.13, beautifully restored. At nearby Strēlnieku 4a is the mag-

A splendid Art Nouveau building on Alberta Street.

ST JOHN

Latvia shares with its Estonian and Lithuanian neighbours a great attachment to celebrating the summer solstice, the Feast of St John. At night, great bonfires are lit, around which families and friends gather to drink, sing and dance. A cheese is prepared and beer brewed especially for this festivity. And people don magnificent crowns of wildflowers or oak-leaves—the latter an honour traditionally reserved for men bearing the name of Janis. Flowers said to bloom from ferns only during this one night bring wish for happiness and love. The holiday is also the occasion for great festivals of song and folk-dancing.

nificent building now housing the Riga branch of the Stockholm School of Economics.

Outside the City

Before going out to the beaches on the coast, take a look at two museums just outside of town.

Motor Museum

At the heart of the residential suburbs east of the city at Sergeja Eizenšteina Street 6, the Motor Museum *(Rīgas motormuzejs)* possesses an exception collection of over 100 vehicles from the Soviet Union and captured from the Germans in World War II. Among the highlights are Stalin's 1949 armour-plated Zis, one of 12 identical models that he sent off in different direction whenever he travelled in one of them; Leonid Brezhnev's (wrecked) Rolls Royce, Hermann Goering's Horch 853, the 1936 Jaguar SS100 of Stalin's son, Vasili, not forgetting an 1899 Stoewer, the oldest car preserved by the Soviet Union.

Open-Air Museum

At little further east at Beri, Latvia's open-air folklore museum *(Latvijas etnogrāfiskais brīvdabas muzejs)* presents an ensemble of some 120 18th- and 19th-century wooden houses brought from all over the country to these vast pinewoods on the shore of Lake Jugla. A church, windmill, farmhouses and artisans' dwellings recreate Latvian life of yesteryear. On summer weekends, artisans and folk groups demonstrate traditional activities.

Jūrmala

The pine-wooded gulf coast west of Riga is lined with 30 km of wide sandy beaches. Broken up into green and pleasant neighbourhoods and old fishing villages, the Jurmala resort is laid out on a long strip of land that forms a spit separating the River Lielupe and Lake Babītes from the Gulf of Riga. This high-class holiday resort from the end of the 19th century, reputed for its mellow, healthy climate, therapeutic mud baths and sulphur springs, duly became a favoured destination for the Soviet *nomenklatura*. If this era gave rise to its blockhouse-like hotels, Jūrmala also preserves numerous older, often sumptuously ornate wooden houses. Some of them are now museums displaying the work of Latvian artists or intellectuals. Pollution closed it down after independence, but Jūrmala has been largely cleaned up and renovated. If its water quality is not yet completely up to scratch, the pleasures of idle *dolce farniente*, beach and sporting activities and the Aviary amusement park once again attract crowds of bathers.

Spreading across the centre and north of the country, the Vidzeme region was once shared between two tribes, the Letts of Baltic origin and the Livs, a Finno-Ugric people closely related to the Estonians living along the coast of the Gulf of Riga. The region was repeatedly broken up by occupying powers. Today its bucolic character attracts its more peaceful foreign visitors, in particular to the valley of the River Gauja. On its fringes, in the village of Dikļinear Valmiera, the first Song Festival, in 1866, launched the re-awakening of national awareness.

From Riga to the Estonian border, the highway runs parallel to the coast of the gulf, mostly at a distance. In the summer, the wooded country attracts quite a few visitors to its beaches. But the region's real charm is to be found in the interior, above all in the valley of the Gauja, Latvia's longest river (460 km).

Gauja Valley

The Gauja rises in the southern uplands of the Vidzeme, describing an almost complete loop before flowing into the gulf north of Riga. On its lower course between high banks and wooded hills, the Gauja Valley forms a great national park. Much appreciated by adepts of canoeing and rafting, the river alternates long stretches of calm waters with rapid sections that are short but often turbulent.

Sigulda

The charming landscapes of the area around the town of Sigulda, a major centre of Germanic activity in the Middle Ages, have made it one of the country's most popular destinations for foreign visitors.

Once the land of the Livs, the region was shared from 1207 between the Sword Brethren on the left bank and the Bishop of Riga (and his archbishop successors) on the right bank. Near the present-day town centre up on the high bank overlooking the Gauja, the knights built their castle, not completed until 1226. Largely destroyed in the Great Northern War of 1700, it remains an eloquent ruin. It offers a good view over the river and, in the distance, the brick turrets of the archbishops' Turaida Castle.

Krimulda Castle

On the opposite bank, Krimulda Castle was built on a hillock a few years after that of the Sword

Brethren, but only a few ruined walls now remain, swallowed up by the forest. The best way to see them is to take the cable car across the river, 40 m above the waters. Hikers follow the path starting just after the Gauja bridge.

Two Caves

Hollowed out of the nearby cliff bordering the valley, the little Gutman Cave (*Gutmaņa Ala*) is known as the setting for the dramatic fate that befell Maija, the tragic Rose of Turaida. The walls are covered with inscriptions left by travellers and lovers, the oldest dating back to the 17th century. A short walk away, the Viktor Cave (*Mazā Ala*) bearing the name of Maija's beloved is even smaller. The way back to the upper plateau is up a stairway of 400 steps—or by the road.

Turaida Castle

High point of any visit to Sigulda, the archbishops' Turaida Castle (*Turaidas Pils*) is perched on a slope overlooking the Gauja. The redbrick structure of 1214 replaced an ancient wooden bastion of the Livs. It lost its strategic importance after the Livonian War (1558–82) and went up in smoke in 1776. Extensively restored—too much so for some tastes—it has preserved a main tower from the top of which you get a spectacular view over the fortifications and the curves of the River Gauja. Another building houses an exhibition of the castle's history and that of the Livs: jewels, weapons, reconstitutions of historic events and daily life retrace the history of the Liv tribes forcibly converted to Christianity and assimilated to the dominant culture.

THE ROSE OF TURAIDA

One of Latvia's most popular legends, inspired by a real event, involves the young orphan Maija taken in and educated by the secretary of Turaida Castle. She grew into a young woman of great beauty and fell in love with the castle gardener, Viktor. One day, when the country was at war, she was confronted with the forceful advances of a Polish deserter. Refusing to yield to him, she invented a fateful subterfuge: in exchange for her liberty, she promised the soldier her magic scarf to protect him against wounds in battle. To convince him of its effectiveness, she persuaded him to strike her with his sword—and collapsed, her honour safe. The soldier was found the next day and hanged. As for Maija, dead at 19, she became a symbol of purity and true love.

Before reaching the castle, you pass by one of Latvia's oldest wooden churches (1750). Close by, at the foot of an old lime tree, is the solitary tomb of the Rose of Turaida (1601–20), where newlyweds traditionally come with their bouquets of flowers. Behind the church is a sculpture garden depicting the themes of traditional Latvian folksongs.

Latvian Animal Park

Some 15 km from Sigulda (direction Līgatne), the Latvian Animal Park has assembled a cross-section of the region's animals in vast enclosures. The park is popular with children and also organizes group activities.

Cēsis

Further upstream from Sigulda, the little town of Cēsis is the second landmark of the Gauja Valley. Integrated into the valley's national park, it has preserved some of the buildings that bear witness to its historic role as a bastion of the Livonian Order.

Castle

With its walls open to the skies, its tower and keep, the Livonian Knights' fortress presents one of the country's most evocative castle ruins. It was built in the early 13th century. The most impressive view is from the surrounding park laid out around a pond and Russian Orthodox church (1845). Access to the park is through the town's History and Arts Museum housed in the new castle (built in 1777). In tracing the history of the town and its region, the museum collections include finds from excavations on the castle site and its surroundings, notably beautiful medieval jewels found in tombs. From the top of the Ladermacher Tower, there is a fine view over the ruins and the neighbouring St John's Church.

Town Centre

Dominating the town centre, St John's Church (*Jāna Baznīca*) was consecrated in 1287. Now Lutheran, the Gothic edifice has since been frequently modified. Its 15th–17th century tombstones of Livonian Knights are for the most part badly disfigured. Nearby Rīgas Street is the town's main shopping thoroughfare. The most noteworthy buildings are the Seller House (1788) at No. 16 and the Town Hall (1767) at No. 7, its façade decorated with the town's coat of arms, a knight in armour defending the castle.

Lielstraupe Castle

About 25 km to the west, the small town of Straupe was a member of the Hanseatic League in the 14th century. From this prosperous past it has preserved the fine Lielstraupe Castle, attrac- 53

tively located above the River Brasla. Founded in the 13th century, it was later rebuilt in Baroque style.

Valmiera

At the northern boundary of the Gauja National Park, Valmiera lies along a sharp bend in the river. Badly damaged in World War II, the town has preserved its Lutheran Church of St Simon (*Sīmana Baznīca*), one of the older churches of the Latvian countryside consecrated in 1283. It was renovated in 1739, after burning down in the Great Northern War. A network of staircases climb to the top of the belltower, some 50 m above the city centre and river. Right up against the church are the ruins of a Livonian castle, just a few fragments of the walls and foundations. A small folk museum is of local interest, and an observation platform offers a view over the Gauja.

Mazsalaca

Less than 20 km from the Estonian border, the town of Mazsalaca is worth a visit for its pretty park stretching along the banks of the River Salaca. From the Valtenburg Manor (1780), 2 km from the centre of town, the Skaņais

Turaida Cstle, the highlight of a visit to Sigulda.

Kalns track (for hikers, cyclists or motorists) continues another 3 km to groups of wooden sculptures scattered around a beautiful forest—gnomes, knights, animals and legendary characters of medieval folklore.

Pleasant picnic sites have been laid out on the banks of the Salaca high above the river flowing gently between pinetrees and leafy greenery at the foot of red limestone cliffs.

The Northeast

Landscapes in the northeast of Vidzeme are slightly more hilly than the rest of the country—its Mount Gaizinkalns (311 m) is the highest peak in Latvia—but the region attracts relatively few visitors. Among its main points of interest is the town of Alūksne, known for its Bible Museum honouring Johann Ernst Gluck, first translator of the Bible into Latvian in the 18th century. The Otte open-air museum, located near the River Paparze on the way to Gulbene, recreates the atmosphere of a traditional farm of the region, with a barn, wheat granary and above all a windmill built in 1785 and still in working order.

To the south, Cesvaine boasts a castle built in 1897 (now a school) fashioning a fake medieval look with an astonishing mixture of architectural styles.

◤ LATGALE
Daugava Valley, Land of the Blue Lakes

Latgale spreads out on both sides of the River Daugava, stretching from Riga far down to the southeast corner of the country. Bordering on Russia and Belarus, the region was long part of the Polish kingdom (1561–1772), and ever since that era it has formed the main Catholic bastion of Latvia. The most elevated part of the area is known as the "Land of the Blue Lakes".

Hung and dried: such is the fate of the fish from the blue lakes.

Daugava Valley
All along the Daugava Valley, a natural route for access to the interior, winding between the edges of Vidzeme to the north and Zemgale to the south, towns and villages have often developed at the confluence with smaller rivers.

Recalling the time when the region was divided into several earldoms, many towns still feature the ruins of Livonian fortresses, all in various states of repair—notably Lielvārde, Aizkraukle, Koknese (partly submerged) and Krustpils.

Two museums devoted to major figures of Latvian literature are well worth a visit.

Lielvārde

The Andrejs Pumpurs museum celebrates the late 19th-century author of epic poetry recounting the myth of Lāčplēsis, a popular folk-hero, half man, half bear. It stands in a park peopled with wooden statues illustrating his epic themes.

Aizkalne

A long way upstream near Dunava, the town is home to the museum of poet Jānis Rainis, the country's most renowned writer. It details his struggle against political and social oppression at the turn of the 20th century, including his deportation to Siberia and exile in Switzerland. Champion of Latvian statehood, he was a member of parliament and minister during the short period of national independence in the 1920s.

Daugavpils

The country's second-largest city (population 108,000), close to the Lithuanian and Belarusian frontiers, is heavily industrial, without great attractions for the visitor apart from the gigantic Russian fortress of 1810. This lone vestige of the city's past has come to symbolize Daugavpils' important Russian-speaking majority (over 60 per cent) resulting from the Soviet immigration after World War II.

Krāslava

Upstream, the Daugava winds between high river banks, some of them reaching 40 m, as here at Krāslava. The lavish Baroque interior of the town's 18th-century Catholic church has 12 altars.

Land of the Blue Lakes

The true religious centre of Latgale is further north at Aglona. A Catholic basilica and convent were erected near the village in the late 18th century, before the territory was seized by the Russians. They remained pilgrimage centres for the Feast of Assumption and were restored in 1993 for the visit of Pope John Paul II.

It is there that the "land of the blue lakes" begins, a picturesque region in which the lakes nestle amid wooded hills. In the triangle formed by Aglona, Krāslava and Ezemieki, there are nearly 300 lakes, small and large. The most beautiful is no doubt Lake Ezezers (Hedgehog), with its 36 isles and islets and rugged banks scalloped with countless little bays.

Further north, Lake Razna, set among the hills, is the second-largest in Latvia. At mostly Russian-speaking Rēzneke there's a museum of history and culture. 57

In the centre of the country between Riga and Lithuania, the little region of Zemgale is largely agricultural and, today as in the past, the most prosperous in Latvia. It was the last territory to yield to the Livonian Knights, at the end of the 13th century, and was incorporated in 1561 into the independent duchy of Courland (which included present-day Kurzeme).

Bauska Castle

Up on its promontory 68 km south of Riga, the castle overlooks the River Mēmele just before it flows into the Lielupe. Built by the Livonian knights in the middle of the 15th century to strengthen their control over Zemgale, it has been many times destroyed and restored. You can still distinguish the remains of the medieval castle, its redbrick walls and tower, from the more recent castle, better preserved, of the dukes of Courland. One restored wing of the older castle now houses a museum devoted to Bauska's history.

Rundāle Palace

Less than 15 km to the west is Rundāle Palace, a Baroque and Rococo gem surrounded by vast French-style gardens.

In 1734, the ambitious Count Ernst Johann Biron, Prime Minister and favourite of Russia's formidable Empress Anna Ivanovna, had his summer palace designed by Bartolomeo Rastrelli (1700–71), the celebrated Italian architect of the Winter Palace in St Petersburg. Artisans came from all over Europe to this godforsaken corner of Zemgale, reinforced by platoons of Russian soldiers. On the death of his protectress in 1740, Biron was sent into exile and the palace construction was abandoned. It was many years before Catherine the Great gave the count back his title, and Rastrelli returned in 1764 to finish off the job he had begun 30 years earlier.

Conceived with its grounds along a symmetrical axis of 2 km, the château designed in warm colours stands behind a vast courtyard, offering a quite stunning perspective on arrival. Crystal chandeliers, silk wall covering, stucco work by the team of Berlin artist Johann Michael Graff, Italian frescoes, no expense was spared. All the rooms that are open to visitors have been refurnished in the Rococo style of the 1760s. (The original furnishings were carried off in 1795 by Duke Pierre, son of Ernst Johann,

Sumptuous Rundāle Palace is often compared to Versailles.

to his Silesian castle at Sagan when Courland lost its independence.) Among the most impressive of the château's 138 rooms are the Throne Room with its mirrors, gilt and Italian-style painted ceiling, the exquisite White Hall that served as a ballroom, and the Grand Gallery banquet hall.

In the third wing is an exhibition devoted to the history of the palace and the dukes of Courland. The ground floor houses a museum of decorative arts and furniture from the 16th to 19th centuries, with an annex at the entrance for a museum of religious art.

Take a walk in the gardens, with their great avenues of box trees, pavilions and fountains.

Jelgava

About 35 km from the palace, the great industrial town of Jelgava was the capital of the duchy of Courland for more than two centuries. In the 17th and 18th centuries Jelgava was an important cultural centre, and it has preserved a Baroque palace designed by Bartolomeo Rastrelli, even bigger than Rundāle, and the family tomb of the dukes of Courland. Their palace, undergoing renovation, at present houses the Latvian Agriculture Academy. 59

Maritime in the west, with a coastline 360 km long, the country opens onto the Gulf of Riga and the Baltic Sea. Inland, woods and forests dominate the landscape. Traditionally shared between the Finno-Ugrian Livs and the Baltic Couronians, the region joined up with neighbouring Zemgale in 1561 to form the Duchy of Courland, and immediately prospered. In 1651, Duke Jacob tried his hand at colonization by purchasing an African island in the Gambian delta, and Tobago in the Antilles. The territory was incorporated into Russia in 1795. At some distance from the major highways, it is sparsely populated, except for the thousands of storks in summer.

Northern Towns

The smaller towns of the region all seem to conform to the same pattern: an old centre with a few wooden houses, an old church in Germanic style, with a sturdy square tower topped by a spire and, quite often, a gallery projecting midway over the nave, a museum of local history, not forgetting the bourgeois manors of centuries past, and ruined castles of Livonian knights. A typical example is Tukums, with its Lutheran church dating from

1644, the neoclassical Castle of Durbe (1820) and the red-brick hunting lodge of Jaunmoku (1901), with an Art Nouveau air about it. Built 6 km west of town for a former mayor of Riga, it now houses a small natural history museum.

Milzkalne

At Milzkalne, 5 km northwest of Tukum, you can visit Šlokenbeka, the last surviving example of a 15th-century fortified Baltic manor, built by Werner von Butler, a vassal of the German Order. It has been rebuilt several times, and extensions added. After its most recent restoration it serves as the Latvian Road Museum.

Jaunpils

This town 30 km to the south has one of the few castles of the Livonian Order that is not in ruins. Built in 1301, it was ceded by the Order to Count Thies von de Recke in 1559, and it remained in his family until 1922. The exterior is much the same as when it was first built, but the inside has been modified, apart from the arcaded courtyard.

See the Lutheran church next door (1592), with a high altar and pulpit dating from the 17th century, as well as the mill (1816),

Kandava and Sabile

Further west, Kandva and Sabile were both founded in the pretty Abava Valley. The former is worth a detour for its big white Lutheran church (1736) overlooking the town. It has a Baroque pulpit. The latter was an important wine-growing town until the 17th century, with what may be the world's northernmost vines, of which a few remain to this day. On the other side of the Abava, the Pedvāle Open-Air Art Museum exhibits abstract sculpture and various creative works.

Talsi and Dundaga

Different town, same story: Talsi, the economic centre of the north of Kurzeme, has a fine church dating from 1567, and several old houses. The large village of Dundaga, 35 km to the northwest, is known for its grand castle founded around the middle of the 13th century, said to be haunted by the ghost of the Green Virgin, walled up alive for misbehaving.

The Coast

On the shores of the Bay of Riga, bordered by long beaches trimmed with pine forest, the villages of the herring fishermen seem lost in time. At Kolka Point, the gulf opens onto the Baltic opposite the Estonian island of Saaremaa. Beyone the orange sun-shaped monument, the strong currents flowing through the straight have created a reef 6 km long. When tempests rage, great breakers, up to 7 m high, crash onto the shore.

Slītere National Park

The peninsula is an important migration zone and is part of the Slitere national park, stretching along the Liv coast at the edge of the strait. It is reputed for its biodiversity and can be resumed in a few words: dunes, fauna, and primeval forest, crossed by the coastal track. Between Gipka and Oviši, 14 Liv fishing villages have been listed, including Kosrags, with its 18th-century wooden houses. At Vaide, you can visit a most unusual museum *(Ragu Kolekciza)*: a forest warden's personal collection of deer horns and antlers, some bearing the scars of attack by wolves. At Mazirbe, the House of the Livs illustrates their culture.

Ventspils

Latvia's main port, Ventspils, despite its industrial role, has maintained a certain harmony in the centre, with its cobblestone streets and restored old houses. On the left bank of the Venta, a fine German Lutheran church of 1835 stands near a market and several Art Nouveau buildings (on Pils Street). The Ventspils Museum has taken up quarters in

the Castle of the Livonian Order at 17 Jana Street. Built in the 13th century, it has been remodelled and renovated to house the museum collections.

Ventspils has an inviting beach awarded the blue flag of excellence. You can walk out on the long jetties closing the entrance to the port. Visit the interesting Open-Air Fishing Museum, 2 Rinku Street, displaying fishermen's houses, anchors, boats, tools and a mill.

Kuldīga
Upriver along the Venta, the little town of Kuldīga is, with its wooden houses, the most picturesque in Kurzeme, though perhaps a little faded. Capital of the Duchy of Courland from 1561 to 1573, more village than town, it shows off what finery it has around Rātslaukums Square. At no 7 stands the oldest wooden house of the province (1670) and at no. 5 an old Town Hall of the same period, also made of wood.

On Liepījas Street there's a superb restored 18th-century granary. If you follow Raina Street, opposite, you will reach the Catholic Church of the Holy Trinity (Sv. Trīsvīenthas baznīca), consecrated in 1640 and known for its

Soft sands along the coast of Courland.

handsome sober Baroque interior. The main altar was a gift of Tsar Alexander I.

North of the square, the Lutheran Church of St Catherine (Sv. Katrina baznīca) was rebuilt in 1672 after a fire and, level with the bridge of the river Alekspīte, a mill dating from 1807. Just above it, the site of the old castle of the Livonian Knights destroyed during the war of the north, is occupied by a pleasant sculpture garden.

Behind the guard's house (1735), the District Museum, displaying fine bronze swords and jewellery from the late Middle Ages) is set in a wood and stone house that housed the Russian pavilion during the World's Fair of 1900 in Paris. It overlooks the Venta River, dammed by the "falls" of the Kuldigas Ruma, in fact a ledge 1–2 m high but stretching over 250 m.

Liepāja
The journey through Kurzeme ends at Liepāja, in the southwest of the country. The third-largest town of Latvia, set on a wide coastal spit separating the sea from two lakes, the city is mostly industrial. However, you can see a few Art Nouveau buildings, a History and Art Museum, and, in the 18th-century Church of the Holy Trinity, believed to be the biggest organ in Europe.

Dining Out

Largely influenced by the cooking of Germany, Russia and Poland, Latvian cuisine is based on seasonal produce prepared in the traditional manner. Without gourmet pretensions, it can be flavourful, as exemplified by the excellent *rupjmaize* rye bread omnipresent with all meals. (Note that in some restaurants, the strict order of dishes may not be respected for the whole table, so that one person may still be eating a starter when other guests are being served their desserts.)

Soups *(zupas)* are a staple feature of most menus, for instance *hapukapa* made from sauerkraut, mutton and vegetable soup, or chilled soup *(aukstāzupa)*.

Another Latvian favourite is smoked or marinated fish, notably tender herring served with potatoes and sour cream or in a salad with beetroot, gherkins or apples and onions *(rossolye)*. Salmon roe is the Latvians' "red caviar" *(sarkanie ikri)*, excellent on toast or blinis.

You'll find all kinds of salads, for example tongue *(mēle)* with mayonnaise, spices or marinated in red wine.

Among the meat dishes, the favourite is pork *(cūkgaļas)* served as thinly sliced scallops *(karbonāde)*, charcoal-grilled kebabs *(šašlik)* or chops. Other possibilities include beef steak *(liellopu gaļas)*, often with onions; chicken *(putna gaļas)* "cordon bleu" stuffed with cheese and ham and coated in breadcrumbs, smoked *(kupināta vista)* or in a sour cream sauce; mutton *(jēra gaļas)* grilled or in kebabs; and also rabbit or hare and—much appreciated by Latvians—roast goose stuffed with apples and plums.

Fish is most often grilled: sturgeon *(store)*, carp *(carpas)*, salmon *(lasis)*, trout *(forele)*, herring *(siļķe)* and eel *(zuši)*. They are served with mushrooms, vegetables and potato pancakes *(kartupaļu pankūciņas)*.

Choice of desserts is best in late summer, when the forest's wild berries are picked and baked in tarts. You find all kinds of pancakes *(bliny)* and cakes, often creamy—though that is not the case with *rupjmaizes kārtojums*, a layer cake of rye breadcrumbs, jam and cream.

Beer is the national drink (look for Aldaris), way ahead of vodka. As for black Balsam, a plant liqueur with 45° alcohol content and a rather special taste, it's best drunk with after-dinner coffee.

Shopping

As in the other Baltic States, craftwork is the major source of products for gift shops and souvenir stalls. Wood is a time-honoured material for hard-wearing toys and kitchen utensils (especially, finely carved spoons). You will also find the ever-popular *matryoshka* nesting dolls, made in Russia.

Leather is made into all kinds of articles such as wallets and handsome book-jackets. Ceramics of good quality are crafted for vases, beer mugs and candlesticks.

Also quite prominent are dolls in regional costume and decorative stained-glass depictions of folklore scenes of daily life, fruits or animals.

Fabrics present a wide range of choices—finely woven linen, embroidered table runners that will last a lifetime, blouses and Latvian costume, as well as felt berets and bonnets. Scandinavian-style Jacquard pullovers are knitted here in traditional Latvian patterns symbolizing the sun, fertility, good fortune, etc. Many elderly ladies make pin-money by hand-knitting socks gloves and stocking

caps—some of them up to 1 m in length.

Amber, which you may be able to find washed up on the beaches of Courland after the autumn storms, is the favoured material for jewellery. From a simple necklace of rough chunks of amber to a refined jewel set in silver, you will find a very varied choice in an endless range of colours—from white to black through yellow, orange and even green. Animal figurines may also be carved in amber.

Another, more hospitable option: take home a bottle of black Balsam. This liqueur is produced in Riga using 24 sorts of herbs, roots and flowers and can be bought in attractive ceramic pitchers in several sizes.

The Hard Facts

Airport
Riga Airport is located 8 km southwest of the city centre. Besides taxis, the No. 22 bus runs every 20 to 30 minutes.

Currency
Until Latvia adopts the Euro (planned for 2010), the unit of currency is the *lats* (LVL) divided into 100 *santīmi* with coins from 1 to 50 *santīmi*, 1, 2 and 100 *lats*, and notes from 5 to 500 *lats*.

Money can be changed at Riga Airport (6 a.m.–10 p.m.), the main railway station (8.30 a.m.–9.30 p.m.), or in exchange bureaux, which offer the best rates, compared with banks or hotels.

The use of credit cards has spread rapidly, particularly for withdrawing cash from ATMs.

Electricity
220 Volts, 50 Hz; continental European-style two-pin plugs are used.

Opening Hours
Shops open from 9 or 10 a.m. to 5 or 6 p.m., often with a lunch break. Some shops, especially those selling food, have longer hours.

Telephone
Phone cards distributed by Lattelekom (2, 3 or 5 *LVL*) are sold wherever you see the sign *Telekarte*.

To call abroad, dial 00, the country prefix (1 for USA and Canada, 44 for UK) and local number omitting the initial 0. Most of the country is now equipped with modern phones, but a few places with only 6-digit numbers require you to dial an initial 1 before dialling the rest of the number.

Time
Latvia's standard time is GMT+2 from November to March and GMT+3 from April to October. When it is noon in London, it is 2 p.m. in Riga.

Tipping
Unknown in the Soviet era, it is becoming much more common to leave a tip. At the restaurant, add 10% to the bill.

Toilets
Women's toilets have an S or D on the door or, as in the other Baltic States, a triangle pointing upwards. Men's toilets have a V or K and triangle pointing downwards.

LITHUANIA

This Way Lithuania

Independence Regained

Believe it or not, Lithuania is plumb in the middle of Europe. Geographers locate the precise centre just 25 km north of Vilnius, the national capital. Once the most powerful of the Baltic States, with its southern borders on the shores of the Black Sea thank to its Polish alliance, Lithuania today occupies no more than a twelfth of its former territory—65,200 sq km—but it's still the largest of the Baltic trio.

The terrain is essentially flat, open on every side to the great European plain that reaches into Poland and Belarus. Its flower-filled meadows are dotted with old wooden farmhouses and traditional haystacks.

Lithuania was founded on the banks of the Neman *(Nemunas)*, its only river flowing to the sea. It forms a great delta on the Baltic, a haven for migratory birds. A lagoon has filled there, separated from the sea by one the world's biggest sand spits, 100 km long. The stretch of dunes, planted with pines, is known as the Amber Coast, or sometimes the "Lithuanian Sahara" and has become once more a popular resort area.

Despite its strong national identity, Lithuania has retained traces of its turbulent past in a population of 3.6 million comprising 83 per cent Lithuanians, more than 6 per cent Russians, nearly 7 per cent Poles and 2.5 per cent Ukrainians and Belarusians. Before World War II, the country also had a very prominent Jewish community—to which could be added an influx of Karaites, a Jewish sect dating back to 1397 when Grand Duke Vytautas brought them from Crimea. They were followed in the 18th century by the Tartars and the Russian Orthodox Old Believers. But he most indelible imprint has been that of Poland—Lithuania can be as romantic and nationalist as its neighbour, which often considered it an integral part of its territory.

The last country in Europe to be converted to Christianity (in the 14th and 15th centuries), it is nevertheless the most religious of the Baltic States, clinging to its fervent Catholic faith. This intense fervour played an important role in Lithuania's national destiny as the first of the Baltic States to affirm its independence from the Soviet Union. In 1988, the national flag was once against hoisted on the Castle of Gedyminas, founder of Vilnius.

Flashback

8th–11th centuries	Tribes in the interior gradually fortify their settlements in order to protect themselves against the regular coastal raids of the Vikings. The name of Lithuania appears for the first time in 1009, in a German chronicle.
13th–14th	The tribal chief Mindaugas presides over the union of several Baltic territories. Submitting to baptism as a Christian, he is crowned first king of Lithuania in 1253, but the pagans regain their hold ten years later. In 1323, Gedyminas, still a confirmed pagan, declares Vilnius the capital of Lithuania. Fearing invasions by the Germanic knights and Muscovites, one of his heirs, Grand Duke Jagellon, seals an alliance with Poland by marrying the young princess Hedwig. He is himself crowned King of Poland two years later (1386) with the name Ladislas II. Converted on this occasion to Catholicism, Lithuania is governed by Grand Duke Vytautas, a cousin of Jagellon. Only the land of the Samogites holds out as pagans, until 1413.
15th–16th centuries	For 200 years, the Jagellon dynasty reigns over a Polish-Lithuanian kingdom enjoying a truly golden era. In 1410, at the Battle of Grünwald, its armies led by Vytautas put an end to the hegemony of the Teutonic Knights in Eastern Europe. At this time, the kingdom forms the biggest state in Europe. On a purely local level, the death of Vytautas in 1430 heralds a slow decline for Lithuania within the state coalition. This becomes a harsh reality with the 1569 Union of Lublin unifying Poland and Lithuania. Originally an independent part of the kingdom, Lithuania is weakened by the extinction of the Jagellon dynasty and reduced to the status of just another province. Polish becomes the official language of Lithuania.
17th–18th centuries	While its neighbours grow in strength, the Polish kingdom experiences a decline. The territory is carved up on three separate occasions between Russia, Austria and Prussia until its disappearance in 1795. The major part of Lithuania becomes Russian. Serfdom is introduced. Polish uprisings against their foreign rulers find a counterpart in Lithuania in 1830 and 1863. A bloody repression drives

many intellectuals into exile in Prussia. Poorer refugees emigrate to America. Russianization is going full throttle. Publications in the Roman alphabet are forbidden. But the episode awakens the national consciousness of the people.

20th century– present

Lithuania is occupied by the Germans in World War I. It proclaims its independence towards the end of the war, on February 16, 1918. By the autumn of 1920, however, Poland's newly reconstituted armed forces invade Vilnius and stay there till 1939. The capital of the young state is consequently moved to Kaunas, while Memel *(Klaipêda)* on the Baltic coast is annexed in 1923.

World War II sees a wave of invasions: Soviet, expelling a million Poles, German in 1941, causing the extermination of over 200,000 people, mostly Jews, in the concentration camps, and Soviet again in 1944. Tens of thousands of Lithuanians are sent to the gulags. Armed struggle continues until 1953. From 1988, public demonstrations protest the Soviet annexation.

On March 11, 1990, Lithuania declares itself independent. In 1998 Valdas Adamkus becomes president. He is re-elected in 2004. The same year, Lithuania joins NATO and the European Union.

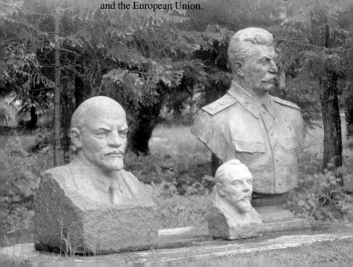

On the Scene

The Old Town districts of Vilnius, among the largest in Eastern Europe, were declared a World Heritage Site by UNESCO in 1994. Not far from the Lithuanian capital, at the heart of an idyllic landscape of lakes, the venerable town of Trakai and its fortress occupy a small island. The northeast of the country is dotted with lakes and well-tended forests. To the south is the region that the Lithuanians have named the "country of song". At the confluence of the rivers Neris and Nemunas, is the university town of Kaunas, with Klaipėda further west, and the coastal spit of Courland.

■▶ VILNIUS AND ITS SURROUNDINGS

Cathedral, Upper Castle, Old Town, City Outskirts, Trakai, Europos Parkas

According to legend, Grand Duke Gedyminas (1275–1341) chose to build his capital here after dreaming that a metal wolf led him to the spot during a hunt in the valley surrounded by rolling hills. This was in 1323, when the grand duchy of Lithuania was still ruled from Trakai, 28 km to the west. The only Baltic capital to be established in the interior, some 300 km from the sea, Vilnius was founded on a hill overlooking the confluence of the broad River Neris and the smaller Vilnia. Apparently inhabited from the end of the 10th century, the site was rapidly fortified after Gedyminas had made his choice: upper and lower castles, with the medieval town developing to the south.

From the 14th century, merchants, craftsmen and clerics, Germans and Jews, came from all over Europe in response to the call of the Grand Duke. One of the largest towns of Eastern Europe in the 15th century, Vilnius attracted the attention of several invaders: Teutonic Knights, Tartars, Russians, Swedes and Poles. The Germans and Soviets fought over the territory in World

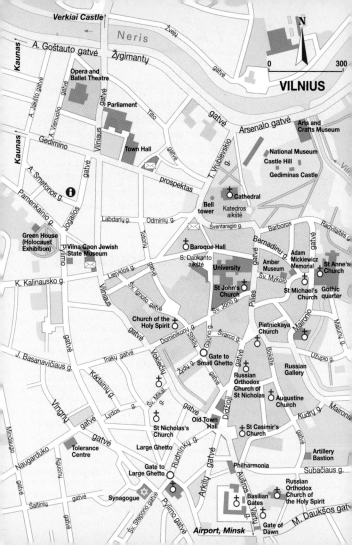

Verkiai Castle

N

Neris

VILNIUS

0   300

Kaunas

A. Goštauto gatvė

Žygimantų

gatvė

Žvejų

A. Jakšto gatvė

gatvė

Opera and Ballet Theatre

Parliament

Tilto

Vilniaus

Arsenalo gatvė

Arts and Crafts Museum

A. Vienuolio

Kaunas

Gedimino

A. Smetonos g.

Town Hall

T. Vrublevskio

gatvė

National Museum

Castle Hill

Gediminas Castle

prospektas

Pamenkalnio g.

Jogailos

Cathedral

Bell tower

Katedros aikštė

Barboros

Green House (Holocaust Exhibition)

Labdarių g.

Odminių g.

Šventaragio g.

Radvilaitės g.

Vilna Gaon Jewish State Museum

Tilto

Totorių

Baroque Hall

S. Daukanto aikštė

Bernardinų

Amber Museum

Adam Mickiewicz Memorial

St Anne's Church

K. Kalinausko g.

Liejyklos g.

University

Sv. Mykolo

St Michael's Church

Gothic quarter

Sv. Ignoto gatvė

St John's Church

Pilies

Sv. Jono

Maironio

Malūnų

Vilniaus

Church of the Holy Spirit

Dominikonų

Stiklių

Gaono

Švarco g.

Piatnickaya Church

J. Basanavičiaus g.

Traky gatvė

Vokiečių

Žydų

Gate to Small Ghetto

Boksto

Russian Gallery

Užupio g.

Maironio

Kėdainių

Sv. Mikal.

Lydos

Russian Orthodox Church of St Nicholas

Augustine Church

Kudry g.

Vingrių

gatvė

St Nicholas's Church

Old Town Hall

Didžioji

St Casimir's Church

Mindaugo

Naugarduko

Tolerance Centre

Aguonų

Large Ghetto

Rūdninkų g.

Philharmonia

Artillery Bastion

Subačiaus g.

Šaltinių

gatvė

Gate to Large Ghetto

Synagogue

Sv. Stepono gatvė

Pylimo gatvė

Arklių

Aušros

Bazilijonų

Basilian Gates

Vartų

Russian Orthodox Church of the Holy Spirit

Gate of Dawn

M. Daukšos g.

Airport, Minsk

War II. The vast majority of Jews, nearly 50 per cent of the city's population before 1939, were exterminated. With a population today of 580,000, Vilnius plays a key role between East and West and remains a multicultural city—54 per cent Lithuanian, 20 per cent Polish, 19 per cent Russian, 5 per cent Belarus, just 0.5 per cent Jewish.

Cathedral and Upper Castle

North of the Old Town, where the Lower Castle stood before it was demolished at the beginning of the 19th century, the mighty Cathedral *(Arkikatedra Bazilika)* looks as though it's sailing over the vast ocean of its esplanade. A first church was built here in 1251 after the conversion of Mindaugas, unifier of Lithuania. It was destroyed in the pagan rebellion against Christianity in 1263 and made way for a temple dedicated to Perkūnas, great god of lightning. In 1387, when the duchy had imposed Christianity as its official religion, a cathedral was erected, notably for the coronation of Lithuania's grand dukes. After many transformations, it was rebuilt in neoclassical style in 1801, with a columned porch and a fronton topped by three giant statues of saints: Helen; Stanislas carrying the Cross in the centre; and Casimir, patron saint of Lithuania. In the superb Baroque Casimir's chapel (1636) to the right of the choir, the saint's life is told in frescoes, and his remains are preserved in a silver reliquary placed on the altar. Immediately beneath, notice the portrait revealing the saint with an extra hand holding a lily. The chapel is also decorated with fine silver statues of the kings of Poland and Lithuania.

Belfry

On the cathedral forecourt, the belltower was originally part of the bastions on the Lower Castle's moated ramparts. The bottom tier dates to the 13th century and the upper section to the 16th. The clock was made in Germany and only shows the hours.

Lower Castle

To the right of the Cathedral, a new statue of Grand Duke Gedyminas was erected in 1996. He is clad in full armour, and is leading his horse. Join a guided tour to visit the nearby excavated site of the Lower Castle *(Žemutinės Piljes Muziejus)*. This was the residence of the grand dukes, destroyed by the Russians in the early 19th century.

Gedyminas Castle

From the cathedral square, a stone path climbs gently to the top of the Upper Castle mound. 73

The bastion erected in the 14th century withstood enemy attack for three centuries until it was all but destroyed from 1655 to 1661 during the war against the Muscovites. All that remains is the lower level, open to the skies and overgrown with grass. Pending a planned restoration, at present only the western tower is open to the public—it's the landmark of the city, proudly flying the national flag, which was hoisted here from October 7, 1988, well before the country regained its formal independence.

The tower houses the attractive Upper Castle Museum (*Aukštutinės Pilies Muziejus*) exhibiting medieval weapons and scale models of the castle.

From the roof you get a fine view north to the River Neris and the suburbs and south over the Old Town and the Cathedral. To the east you look over the River Vilnia, half-hidden by the trees on its banks, and the hill of the Three Crosses, which were erected in memory of Franciscan monks crucified on this spot.

National Museum

At the foot of the castle hill on the north side, the National Museum (*Lietuvos Nacionalis Muziejus*) divides into two sets of buildings. The first occupies one of the two wings of the Old Arsenal and houses the Lithuanian History and Ethnography Museum, tracing the history of the country from its earliest Stone Age beginnings to the creation of the Lithuanian state in the 13th century. Among the interesting exhibits, assembled mostly from archaeological excavations, are tools, weapons, gems, ornaments, costumes and a remarkable reconstruction of the tomb of a Stone Age holy man.

The museum's second building, installed in the New Arsenal over on the bank of the Neris, continues the story of the Lithuanian state from the 14th century to the 20th-century independence struggles from 1918 to 1940. An appealing part of the museum collection is the folklore section devoted to various regions of Lithuania.

Museum of Applied and Decorative Arts

This museum (*Taikomosios Dailės Muziejus*) is in the second wing of the Old Arsenal. The building also stages concerts and various other cultural events.

Old Town

From the cathedral square, Cathedral Street (*Pilies gatvė*), completely closed to traffic, cuts right through the Old Town area. Very lively in fine weather with people strolling past its café terraces, restaurants and boutiques, the thoroughfare is at the centre of a network of narrow streets on which you will find the town's principal monuments.

House of Adam Mickiewicz

On the left hand side of Bernardinu Street, at No.11, the house where the Lithuanian-Polish poet Adam Mickiewicz lived in 1822 has been transformed into a small museum (*Mickevičiaus Memorialinis Butas-muziejus*). Personal memorabilia trace the life and work of the writer, an ardent Romantic who contributed to awakening the Polish national consciousness under Russian rule.

St Michael's Church

Close by, St Michael's Church (*Šv. Mykolo Bažnyčia*) was consecrated in 1625 at the behest of Lithuania's great hetman (military commander) Leonas Sapiega, who chose it for his family vault. In 1655, the Cossacks plundered the church, one of the finest examples of Renaissance architecture in Vilnius. Since the Soviet period, it has housed an Architecture Museum (*Architektūros Muziejus*).

St Anne's Church

You can't miss the red towers of St Anne's Church (*Šv. Onos Bažnyčia*), a jewel of 16th-century late-Gothic architecture. Its façade is a veritable lacework of 33 different kinds of brick forming an intricate pattern of curved lines, little spires, turrets and flamboyant arches. Napoleon is said to have dreamed of dismantling it to take it back to Paris. The church backs up against the dilapidated buildings of a monastery (closed by the Russians in 1863) incorporating the Bernardine order's Gothic church (*Bernadinų Bažnyčia*), founded in the 16th century. Nearby is a monumental statue to Adam Mickiewicz.

Amber Museum

On your way back to Cathedral Street (*Pilies gatvė*), take the narrow Šv. Mykolo Street to No. 8, housing the Amber Museum with its own gallery-boutique (*Gintaro Musiejus – Galerija*). The museum collection is superbly displayed in a setting of vaulted cellars dating back to the 15th century, when they served as the craftsmen's workshops. You'll see pieces of raw amber, several with insects embalmed inside, as well as Stone Age amulets and modern jewellery.

University

The lane brings you almost directly to Skapo Street which leads to the Presidential Palace (*Prezidentūra*), a massive neoclassical building of 1832, erected on the site of the bishops' 75 medieval palace. Directly opposite is the main entrance to Vilnius University made up of a large group of houses.

Founded in 1579 by King Stephen Bathory and administered by the Jesuits, it is one of the oldest universities in Eastern Europe. The library includes a collection of about 180,000 old and rare books, with 322 15th-century incunabula and 12,000 publications in the Lithuanian language from the first book, *Catchismus* by M. Mažvydas to the 1918 *Declaration of the Republic of Lithuania*. In the vanguard of the struggle to preserve the Polish identity (Mickiewicz was a student here), the university was closed down by the Russians in 1832 and did not re-open until 1919. Its influence was decisive right up to the independence movement of the 1990s. It comprises 13 faculties linked by courtyards. Visit Pocobuto Court in particular to take a look at the Observatory façade decorated with the signs of the Zodiac. It is directly linked to the heart and soul of the place, the vast cobble-stoned Great Court surrounded by a superb ensemble of stylishly arcaded buildings.

St John's Church

Begun in 1387 on the initiative of Grand Duke Jagellon, St John's Church (*Šv. Jonų Bažnyčia*) stands at the back of the Great Court. In the 16th and 17th centuries, University diplomas were handed out here. The main part of the present building, largely late Baroque, dates from the reconstruction following a series of fire in the 1730s. The Baroque choir contrasts with the rather austere style of the rest of the church.

Catholic Church of the Holy Ghost

A short detour by Universiteto Street, then by Dominikonų gatvė, brings you to the Church of the Holy Ghost (*Šv. Dvasios Bažnyčia*). Founded at the end of the 14th century and rebuilt several times, this Catholic sanctuary is an important meeting place for the Polish community of Vilnius. Active throughout the Soviet era, the church's 18th-century Baroque interior is notable for its rose-hued ceilings with stucco and opulent gilded ornament.

A little to the south, Gaono gatvė was once the heart of the Jewish quarter of Vilnius—transformed into a ghetto in World War II.

Didžioji gatvė

Follow Šv. Jono Street back to Pilies gatvė, then turn right; you will reach a small square given over to a craftware market; it is the start of Didžioji gatvė. At No. 2, the Russian Orthodox

From the tower of St John's Church you get a great view over the Old Town.

church of Paraskovila Piatnick-aya *(Piatnickajos Cerkvė)* is unprepossessing but can at least claim to be the town's oldest (1345). Alexander Pushkin's great-grandfather was baptised here; he was an African slave named Hannibal, given to the Tsar by the Sultan of Turkey. At No. 4, Chodkevich Palace houses a Museum of Lithuanian Painting and Sculpture *(Vilniaus Paveiks-ļu Galerija)*, with works from the 16th to 19th centuries.

Town Hall Square

Continue along Didžioji gatvė which widens out into the long triangular-shaped Town Hall Square *(Rotušė aikštė)*, once the hub of the city's activities. At No. 1, a plaque commemorates the stay here in December 1812 of the great French novelist Stendhal during the retreat from Moscow of Napoleon's army. Among the many handsomely restored houses, see No. 10's façade with its two sturdy atlantes. At No. 12, the Russian Orthodox church of St Nicholas *(Šv. Mikalojaus Cerkvė)* reveals a Byzantine Gothic style with Baroque elements added later.

At the other end of the square, the old neoclassical Town Hall rebuilt in 1799 is now the home of the House of Artists.

St Casimir's Church

South of the square is St Casimir's Church (*Šv. Kazimiero Bažnyčia*) founded in 1604 by the Jesuits following the canonization of Casimir IV (Jagellon). The town's oldest Baroque church has had a turbulent history. When it was converted to the Russian Orthodox cult in the first half of the 19th century, two cupolas were added. With the arrival of the Germans in 19015, it became a Protestant church, then, after a period as a wheat granary, the Soviets turned it into an Museum of Atheism. The sober interior has an ornate Baroque high altar.

Artillery Bastion

On the left, the long Subačiaus Street leads to the Artillery Bastion (*Artilerijos Bastėja*), grafted onto the last reconstructed remains of Vilnius's 17th-century eastern city walls. Armour and historic weapons are exhibited in the bastion's dark brick galleries.

Russian Orthodox Church of the Holy Ghost

Make for the Gate of Dawn Street (*Aušros Vartu gatvė*), perhaps the prettiest of the Old Town, through the garden of the Russian Orthodox Church of the Holy Ghost (*Stačiatikų Šv. Dvasios Cerkvė*), consecrated in 1638. The interior reveals a huge bright green icon-screen, with cupola and ceilings in pink and pastel blue. The remains of three 14th-century saints are preserved and dressed in white for Christmas, black for Lent and red the rest of the year.

Gates of Basilian

Coming to Gate of Dawn Street, opposite the terrace of the very chic late 19th-century Hotel Europa, take a look at the monumental Baroque Gates of Basilian

---

THE JEWS OF VILNIUS

The first Jewish merchants and craftsmen came to Vilnius at the written invitation issued by Gedyminas in the 14th century at a time when pogroms and persecutions were sweeping the rest of Europe. At the beginning of the 20th century they numbered just under half the population of the town, 94% of them perishing in the German concentration camps. Of the 100 synagogues that Vilnius once counted, the only one to survive is at 39 Pylimo Street (1903). To trace the history of the Jews in the capital, visit the small Vilna Gaon Jewish State Museum at 4 Pylimo Street, home of the Jewish Community Centre. A permanent exhibit is planned for the Tolerance Centre at Naugarduko 10/2.

(Bazilijonų Vartai), recently restored. They mark the entrance to a Dominican monastery, also due for reconstruction.

Gate of Dawn

In the opposite direction is St Theresa's Church, with a richly ornate interior. In 1671, its Carmelite nuns had a chapel built above the neighbouring Gate of Dawn *(Aušros Vartai)* to house a sacred 17th-century icon of the Virgin Mary, clad in silver. The icon attracts a great number of pilgrims, in particular the Polish.

The gate is the only one remaining of the ten ancient entrances through the Vilnius ramparts. It is from the exterior that you get the best view of its Renaissance upper wall (attic) decorated with the arms of medieval Lithuania and with sculpted head of Hermes, Greek god of merchants.

City Outskirts

The skyline west of the Old Town bristles with church steeples and towers, most of them in dire need of restoration—notably St Nicolas Church (1320), Lithuania's oldest.

Museum of Lithuanian Art

In Viniaus Street, the little 17th-century Radvilos Palace houses the Museum of Lithuanian Art *(Lietuvos Dailės Muziejus)* exhibiting in large part, despite its name, foreign paintings and sculpture.

Museum of the Victims of Genocide

To the north, the new town began to expand in the 19th century around the great Gedimino Prospektas Avenue, lined with the main governmental and other public buildings. On Lukiškių aikštė (previously Lenin Square) facing a small park is the great neoclassical palace that was once the headquarters of the German Gestapo and then the Soviet KGB. Today, it houses the Museum of the Victims of Genocide *(Genocido Aukų Muziejus)*, in their vast majority Lithuania's Jewish population. Former prisoners conduct guided tours around the cells in the basement, left practically unchanged.

Further along are the monumental Soviet National Library and the modern Parliament.

Television Tower

Further west of the centre, in the suburb of Karoliniškés, the 326-m Television Tower *(Televizijos Bokštas)* soars above clusters of low-cost apartment blocks. The tower became a national symbol after Russian troops attacked it on January 13, 1991, killing 13 civilians in the assault. A lift takes you up to a panoramic restaurant.

Trakai Castle stands on an island in Lake Galvė.

St Peter and St Paul Church

To the east of Gedyminas Hill, you will discover Vilnius' finest example of Baroque architecture. The construction of St Peter and St Paul Church (*Šv. Apaštalų Petro ir Povilo Bažnyčia*) was begun in 1668 by Lithuania's great hetman Michael Casimir Pac.

Behind its somewhat austere façade is a quite astonishing interior in which the walls are decorated with some 2000 depictions of Biblical, mythological and historical figures, battle scenes in fresco, stucco and carved relief. Italian masters directed a team of 200 artists in the decoration of this masterpiece of ardent piety.

Even in what were for the faithful the darkest hours of the Soviet era, the church was always open to worshippers.

Trakai

Lithuania's ancient capital lies 28 km west of Vilnius. Fortified in the 14th century, Trakai was built on a long peninsula separating two lakes at the heart of a national historical park bearing its name.

Trakai Castle

Cross over a wooden footbridge to reach the castle, set on one of the 21 islets in Lake Galvė, to the north. It presents a timeless image with its redbrick walls and four massive towers, nicely restored, reflected in tranquil waters plied by yachts, small boats and pedalos. Originally a fortress, the castle became a summer residence for the Grand Dukes and the setting for celebrations after victory over the Teutonic Knights in 1410. Left in a state of neglect from the end of the 15th century, it was many times dismantled and reconstructed. The fine vaulted halls and a building in the castle's second precinct house Trakai's History Museum, in which are displayed the finds of local excavations and other historic memorabilia.

Pusiasalio Castle

Follow the lakeshore to the south and you will come across a second castle (Pusiasalio Pilis) built at the same time by Grand Duke Kestutis to rebuff the Teutonic Knights. From its wooded mound, the castle once dominated the peninsula between Lake Galvé and Lake Luka. It was ravaged by several fires, and today only the rampart walls and bastions remain.

Folk Museum

Return by Karaimų Street, running parallel to the lakeshore and lined with gaily painted wooden houses. At No. 22, the little Karaime Folk Museum tells the story of the Karaite community through utensils and implements of everyday life, weapons and photographs. The Jewish sect, opposed to the Rabbinic tradition and living in Crimea, was enlisted by Grand Duke Vytautas in 1397 for his personal protection and to guard his castle.

Nearby at No. 30 is the 18th-century kenessa, the Karaites' house of worship.

Europos Parkas

North of Vilnius, 19 km along the road to Molėtai, a signpost points to a renowned Central European open-air sculpture museum. It was founded in 1991, in a forest setting, by the Lithuanian sculptor Gintaras Karosas, and covers an area of 55 ha. The museum displays 70 contemporary works of art by Lithuanian and international artists.

The Centre of Europe

About 4 km north of the intersection, another signpost indicates the Geographical Centre of Europe, as defined by the French National Geographical Institute in 1989 (25°19′ longitude, 54°54′ latitude). You have to look hard to locate the spot, marked by a big rock bearing an inscription. To get to it, climb the hill up to the crucifix and come down the other side to find it just beyond a tiny little bridge.

Northeast of Vilnus, meadows and forest, old villages and lakes fringed by reeds form a picturesque landscape.

Labanoro Park

In the lake region of Molėtai, get your first overall view of the park from the tower of an old Soviet astronomic observatory perched on a hill. Its less than graceful architecture is amply compensated by the splendid panorama. With the telescope your guide may help you spot a stork on its nest. The Centre has become The Lithuanian Museum of Ethnocosmology *(Leituvos Etnokosmologijos Muziejus)*, a word coined to represent the relationship between mankind and the cosmic world. The exhibition includes an open-air display of mythological symbols, saints, marked stones, sun dials, etc.

Aukštaitija National Park

To the northeast, this national park was founded in 1794 and covers more than 300 sq km in a magnificent pine and birch forest. The Ice Age bequeathed an

astonishing area of 126 lakes, most of them linked by rivers and channels opening up a vast region of exploration to canoers, campers and fishermen. The two main lakes are Baluošas to the north, with its seven islands and shores surrounded by forest, and the smaller and more developed Lūšia to the south. You'll get an appealing view over the park from the top of Ledakalnis Hill. Many of the park's villages, their wooden houses nestling in the forest clearings, have been declared "ethnographic heritage sites". The most notable are Šuminai, Strazdai and Ginučia, which has a charming restored 19th-century watermill. At Stripeikai, visit the small cabin housing a Bee-Keeping Museum, while in Palūšė, see the wooden Church of St Jospeh (1750) with its free-standing belfry.

East of the park, in stark, decidedly un-idyllic contrast, is the hotly contested Ignalina nuclear power station, said to be identical with that of Tchernobyl and probably due to be closed down in the near future.

The Lithuanians named it *Dainava*, the "country of song". The River Nemunas flows in lazy loops through a landscape of meadows, lakes and pine groves.

Druskininkai

Near the Belarus frontier, the country's main spa resort since the 18th century stretches along the Nemunas' right bank. With its seven mineral springs and ten sanatoriums, the town was greatly expanded in the Soviet era. In the charming centre it has preserved a number of old wooden houses, and a Russian Orthodox church (1865), also of wood, with slender onion domes. Two of the houses have been converted into museums dedicated to two of the town's more famous sons. At 17 Šv. Jokūbo Street, the little Jewish Museum is devoted both to the Druskininkai-born sculptor Jacques Lipchitz (1891–1973) and to the town's Jewish past. At 35 Čiurliono Street is the home and museum of painter-composer M. K. Čiurlionis (1875–1911), who spent a large part of his childhood here. Unadorned or painted wooden sculptures were erected in his memory in 1975 all along the "Čiurlionis Route" from here to his birthplace in Varėna.

Grūtas

A Lithuanian businessman who made a fortune from mushrooms created Grūtas Park *(Grūto Parkas)* on the shore of a lake 7 km from Druskininkai. It comprises an eye-opening collection of Soviet statues: monumental models of all the Soviet Union's great figures dumped on the scrap heap in 1990–91 have found a last resting place here. Marx, Lenin, Stalin, Soviet and Lithuanian heroes and allegories of the Soviet Fatherland are scattered along the path through the forest. The information centre has become a little Soviet museum, with busts of the leaders, official literature, anthems and flags.

Dzūkija National Park

North of Druskininkai, Lithuania's biggest national park covers an area of 560 sq km, 80 per cent of it pinewoods. The River Nemunas winds its way between wooded hills and meadows, across its ancient fluvial-glacial plain. Boat cruises take you to the village of Liškiava overlooking the river, with a particularly fine view from the site of its old castle. The big 17th-century Baroque church is worth a visit; it backs on to an 18th-century monastery and has seven altars.

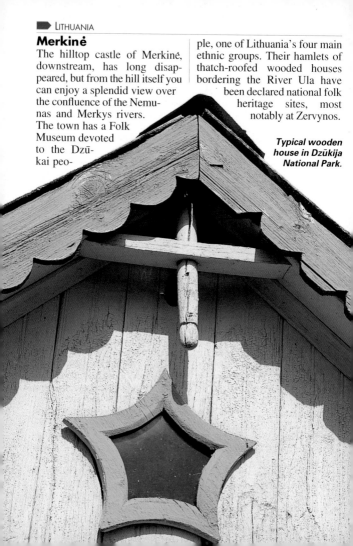

Merkinė

The hilltop castle of Merkinė, downstream, has long disappeared, but from the hill itself you can enjoy a splendid view over the confluence of the Nemunas and Merkys rivers. The town has a Folk Museum devoted to the Dzūkai people, one of Lithuania's four main ethnic groups. Their hamlets of thatch-roofed wooded houses bordering the River Ula have been declared national folk heritage sites, most notably at Zervynos.

Typical wooden house in Dzūkija National Park.

The country's second city (population 361,000), Kaunas developed at the confluence of the Neris and Nemunas rivers. Since the Middle Ages it was a prosperous trading centre, and it became the capital of Lithuania between the two World Wars at a time when Vilnius was occupied by the Polish army. Today a resolutely modern, industrial city, it has nonetheless preserved a small and attractive historical centre.

Old Town

It is there, right beside its two rivers, that the history of Kaunas really began, around the castle erected in the 13th centre to repel the Teutonic Knights. Unfortunately, only one reconstructed tower and a defensive wall still testify to its past grandeur.

Town Hall

A. Jakšto Street leads to the vibrant hub of the medieval city, Town Hall Square (*Rotušes aikštė*), surrounded by handsome brick houses of the 15th and 16th centuries. Built in 1542, the Town Hall (*Kauno Rotušė*), nicknamed the White Swan, combines several architectural styles. Its Baroque pediment adjoins an imposing clock tower rising above the twin towers of the neighbouring 17th-century Jesuit church. Used as a "Wedding Palace" for civil marriage in the Soviet era, it now houses a Ceramics Museum in its vaulted cellars.

Museum of Medical History

Among the many museums surrounding the esplanade, be sure to visit the fascinating Museum of Medical and Pharmaceutical History at No. 28, a 16th-century house. In its cellars are exhibited various medical and surgical instruments, the oldest of them dating back to the 16th century. The museum also incorporates a splendid pharmacy from the 19th century.

Cathedral

Overlooking the corner of the square is the great 15th-century Cathedral of St Peter and St Paul, originally Gothic and redesigned in Baroque style. The opulent interior is decorated with painted ceilings and walls, statues and nine altars, one for each of the nave's pillars.

House of Lightning

Don'tt miss the House of Lightning (*Perkūno Namas*) south of the square near the 15th-century Gothic Vytautas Church, 6 Aleksoto Street. The remarkable red-brick Gothic dwelling has a pediment bristling with spires.

Vilnius gatvé

The Old Town's main thoroughfare, Vilnius gatvé, starts from the foot of the Cathedral. The broad cobblestone street is lined with colourful old dwellings.

Notice in particular the handsome patrician brick mansion at No. 11, declared a historic monument and today housing a bookshop. For the period that Kaunas was the capital of Lithuania, President Antanas Smetona lived further on at No. 33, just beyond the underground passage passing beneath Gimnazijos Street.

New Town

Prolonging the main thoroughfare, the pedestrian Laisvés Avenue crosses the 19th-century part of town from one end to the other. The avenue, nearly 2 km long, is always full of people strolling up and down; it ends at the monumental neo-Byzantine Church of the Archangel St Michael—originally Russian Orthodox and now Roman Catholic.

To the north, on the distinctly Soviet Unity Square (Vienybés Aikšté), the Freedom Monument of 1918 recalls the short-lived glory of Lithuanian independence between the two World Wars. It is always decorated with flowers.

Military Museum

The Military Museum of Vytautas the Great houses a both a huge collection of weaponry and a Museum of Lithuanian History. A separate entrance at the back of the building leads to the M. K. âiurlionis Art Museum, devoted to Lithuanian painting from the 15th to the early 20th century. Be sure to see the remarkable sculpture in tree-bark and trunks by Kaunas-born Elžbieta Daugulienė (1886–1959).

Museum of the Devil

Above Unity Square at 64 Putvinskio Street, an otherwise unprepossessing building houses the truly original Museum of the Devil. Its creator was the artist Antonas Žmuidzinavičius, a prodigious collector who assembled some 260 pieces portraying the Devil, at the turn of the 20th century. The collection in the museum today numbers 1,800 statuettes, ceramics, tobacco pipes, masks, wooden sculpture from Lithuania and the rest of the world.

Pažaislis

Near the artificial Kaunas Lake, 9 km east of town, the Camaldule Order (originating in Camaldoli, Italy, in the 11th century) erected the splendid Pažaislis Convent in the late 17th century. The Baroque ensemble is built around an imposing church whose Italianate façade (1674), flanked by two belfries, was designed by Florentine architects. The great dome rises above pink marble Corinthian columns. The church's stucco, statues and frescoes are also largely the work of Italian painters and sculptors. Plundered by Napoleon's troops in 1812, the Convent was closed after an uprising in 1831 and handed over to the Russian Orthodox Church. It was returned to the Catholic Church in 1992 and is once again inhabited by nuns. Pažaislis is renowned for its classical music concerts organized at the beginning of the summer.

Rumšiškiės

At the far end of Lake Kaunas, 23 km east of town, the Rumšiškiės Open Air Museum *(Liaudies Buitjes Muziejus)* is one of the best in the Baltic States. It covers a vast terrain with more than 140 buildings and annexes from the late 18th to early 20th centuries, transported here from all over the country. The houses are grouped together in coherent units in order to give the impression of veritable villages—enhanced by the activities of craftsmen six months a year.

Standing guard, on a calvary at Rumšiškiės Museum.

Šiauliai

One of the country's larger towns, Šiauliai is worth a visit mainly for its charming Church of St Peter and St Paul (1634) with its tall spire and dazzling white Baroque interior. Nearby is a grand solar clock crowned by a gilded bronze archer, inaugurated in 1986 to commemorate the 750th anniversary of the Battle of Saulė, when the Knights of the Sword Brethren were defeated by the Samogites of Duke Vykintas.

Hill of the Crosses

A major attraction for visitors to the region is the Hill of the Crosses *(Kryžių Kalnas)* about 10 km north of Šiauliai on the Riga highway. The first crosses were set here when the revolts against the Russian rulers in the 19th century. Since then, more than 50,000 more have been planted on this mound: small and simple, huge and elaborate, in wood or in metal, these symbols of the Lithuanians' attachment to the Catholic faith are piled up in a confused mass of crossbeams and the martyred Christ. Each time the Soviet authorities tried to have them removed, they reappeared, popping up in the dead of night, almost as fast as they were taken down. Since the visit of Pope John Paul II in 1993, pilgrims have been coming in ever increasing numbers, especially at Easter.

Žemaitija National Park

In the northwest corner of the country, near the Latvian border, the uplands of Žemaitija, roll gently over hills and meadows. Partly covered by pine forests, the region is dotted with 26 lakes, notably the great Plateliai, broken up into an endless tangle of bays, channels, wooded peninsulas and promontories. The village of Platelai on the northwest side of the lake is at once the park headquarters and a very popular midsummer holiday spot.

Salantai

Before heading for the coast, be sure to stop off at Salantai. On the southern edge of town is the astonishing Orvydas Garden *(Orvidų Sodyba)* created during the Soviet era by the deeply religious sculptor Vilius Orvydas (1852–1992). The themes and variations of this bizarre, mystical

The Hill of the Crosses is a popular place of pilgrimage.

wonderland of grottoes, sculptures, statues, crosses and engraved stones caused the Orvydas family considerable problems during the Communist years.

The Coast

From the Latvian border to the Russian enclave of Kaliningrad, Lithuania's coastline is just under 100 km in length and was a very late addition to the country's territory. After a long series of Viking raids, it fell into the hands of the Germanic Knights in the 13th century, and became part of German Prussia until World War I. The region is of exceptional natural beauty, embracing a vast lagoon into which the River Nemunas flows. The dunes of the huge Courland coastal spit face the Baltic. Since time immemorial, this is where the treasured amber is gathered, washed up by the Baltic waves.

Palanga

The country's main beach resort apparently grew out of a very ancient amber trading port. With its bracing air and a beach stretching 10 km over dunes and pine groves, it has attracted holiday-makers since the 19th century. Once aristocratic in its appeal, Palanga is today very popular with families and the young

AMBER

In the first century AD, Pliny the Elder was already complaining that a tiny piece of amber might cost more than a slave. The middlemen were so numerous on the long route from the shores of the Baltic that nobody knew the origin of amber. For the ancient Balts, it came from the tears of a goddess and the remains of her castle in the sea, destroyed by the God of Thunder Perkūnas to punish her for her forbidden love affair with a simple fisherman. "Baltic gold" is a fossilized pine resin from the forests that covered the region 35 to 50 million years ago. When they were swallowed up in the Eocene Epoch, the amber was washed up by the tides and gradually deposited along the coast, especially between Gdansk and the Baltic States. In these layers deposited on the shore, you may find up to 2.5 kilos of amber per cubic meter of earth. Some pieces have insects embedded within them, testifying to species long extinct. About 250 hues have been identified, ranging from white to black through most of the colours of the rainbow. The largest known piece weighs 9.75 kilos.

The old town of Klaipėda contain many such picturesque buildings.

crowd. It offers all sorts of water sports, beach volleyball and trampoline, therapeutic mud baths and open-air entertainment shows. A favourite promenade takes people out to a long wooden pier facing the centre of the beach, offering a much appreciated view of the sunset.

South of the city centre, French gardener Edouard André laid out a vast park behind the coast at the end of the 19th century. Inside the park, the Tyszkiewicz family of Polish nobles built a palace that is now the Amber Museum *(Gintaro Muziejus)*. Its collection of some 4,500 pieces includes many with insects and plants embedded within the amber, as well as rough chunks weighing several kilos, Stone Age amulets, and jewellery from the Middle Ages to the present day.

Klaipėda

The country's main port and third-largest city (population 189,000), Klaipėda stands at the estuary of the River Danė, opposite the channel separating the lagoon from coastal spit of Courland. For centuries after the foundation of a castle in 1252 by the Livonian Knights, its name was Memel. Thriving from its maritime trade, it came under Prussian rule in 1525, marking that 91

PIONEERING BOATSMAN

Outside Klaipeda's Maritime Museum, you can see the boat of Gintaras Paulionis, the first Balt to row across the Baltic. It took him 16 days to reach Sweden. He disappeared on the return trip, in the same storm that caused the shipwreck of the *Estonia* ferry in 1994.

kingdom's northern frontier. At the beginning of World War I, its population was still half German. After the war, it became a French mandate until it was annexed by Lithuania in 1923.

Damaged in World War II, Klaipėda still preserves in its Left Bank district some of the tile-roofed houses with half-timbered and brick gables typical of old Memel's Germanic *Fachwerk* style.

Theatre Square

Begin your walk on the west side of the Old Town near the river bank of the Danė, where you can see the last remains of the castle of the Livonian Knights.

Nearby, the cobblestone Theatre Square (*Teatro aikštė*) is dominated by the neoclassical theatre (1857). It was from here that Hitler proclaimed the annexation of the region (*Memelland*) in his Third Reich on March 23, 1939.

At the foot of the theatre is a fountain erected in memory of the Memel-born German poet Simon Dach (1605–59), topped by a statue of Ännchen von Tharau, one of his epic heroines.

Half-Timbered Houses

South of the square you will see the finest examples of the town's attractive half-timbered warehouses and mansions, notably the house at 18 Sukilėlįu Street, now a restaurant. Others can be seen on Aukštoji Street, in particular No.3, once the fish market and now converted into an exhibition hall (*Galerija Baroti*).

Museums

At the corner of Didžioji Vandens Street, the History Museum (*Mažovios Lietubos Istorijos Muziejus*) occupies the residence of an 18th-century merchant. Coins, furniture, maps, old photos and finds from archaeological excavations trace the town's story from its origins and its part in Prussian and Lithuanian history.

At the southern end of Old Town on Šaltkalvįu Street, near the covered market, the Blacksmiths Museum (*Kaluystė Muziejus*) exhibits tools and wrought iron objects characteristic of Lithuanian craftsmanship, notably tombstone crosses.

New Town

Built in the 19th and 20th centuries, the New Town district stands on the Danė's right bank. At 12 Liepų Street, the Clocks and Watches Museum (*Laikrodžis Muziejus*) occupies a handsome neoclassical residence of the 19th century.

The neighbouring redbrick building is the Post Office, with magnificent painted interiors where the children of Friedrich Wilhelm III of Prussia found refuge during the Napoleonic military occupation of Berlin. The tower's bells play a concert each Saturday and Sunday at noon.

Almost opposite at No. 7 in a handsome neo-Baroque building is a small folk museum.

Further east, finish off your tour with a walk to the old cemetery, transformed into a sculpture garden (*Mažvydo Parkas*).

Curonian Spit

From the little harbour near the castle, ferries cruise down the River Danė and cross the channel in less than 10 minutes to reach Smiltynė at the northern end of the Curonian (or Courland) Spit.

Nature Museum

From the landing stage is a 1.5-km long promenade (accessible only to minibuses and horse-drawn carriages) facing the port of Klaipėda. Along the way, you will discover the Nature Museum of the Courland Spit (*Kuršių Nerijos Gamtos Muziejus*) shared between three wooden houses. Apart from the area's fauna and flora, the museum deals with the Spit's geological formation and its human activities. Further along, beside old boats in dry dock, is a reconstitution of the living conditions and domestic interiors of a 19th-century fisherman.

Maritime Museum

At the end of the promenade is a Dolphinarium and a 19th-century moated Prussian fort now housing the Maritime Museum (*Jūrų Muziejus*), with its aquarium and nautical collections. From the Smiltynė landing stage, you can take one of the paths through the pine groves to the long wide beach backing on to tall dunes where wild roses bloom in the spring.

Courland National Park

One of the favourite excursions takes you along the whole length of the coastal strip, made a national park (*Kuršių Nerija*) in 1991 and recently declared a UNESCO World Heritage Site. It varies in width from 400 m to 4 km and extends 98 km (50 km in Lithuania) as far as the Russian enclave of Kaliningrad. For nearly 10,000 years, the sand swept by the currents and winds of the Baltic have built up into lofty dunes embracing the Courland lagoon. The strip is somewhat fancifully nicknamed the Lithuanian Sahara, despite the fact that two-thirds of it are covered by beautiful pinewoods inhabited by elk, deer and wild boar.

Located on an important migratory route, the wildfowl are numerous—among them, ducks, swans, eagles and mixed colonies of grey herons and cormorants. If the lagoon shore is covered in reeds, the beach along the Baltic coast is good for swimming.

Villages

Inhabited since time immemorial by fishermen, the peninsula numbers just four villages on its Lithuanian side. Juodkrantė (in Prussian times, Schwarzort), once a major source of amber, was a highly reputable resort in the 19th century. Along its picturesque little fishing harbour is a pleasant promenade bordering the lagoon between sculptures and painted wooden houses. Just above it, the splendid Raganų Kalnas path winds over the Witches' Hill through a beautiful forest of spruce and pine. It is flanked by dozens of wooden sculptures of mythical figures of witches, demons, gnomes and dragons.

The route then bypasses the villages of Pervalka and Preila, moved here in the 19th century after their original locations were buried by the dunes. Vercekrugas, south of Preila, is the tallest dune in the park, over 67 m high.

Nida

Just before the Russian frontier at the edge of a stretch of giant dunes, you come to Nida (formerly Nidden) by the lagoon. Nestling amid the trees, the region's main beach resort (population 2,000) retains the airs and graces of an old fishing village, despite its great popularity. Many of its wooden houses are decorated with elaborate and colourful weathervanes. These were first invented in the 19th century as an identification tag for boats; they were made of tin, painted black and white and had flags at each end.

In search of their past history, many German tourists seek out the house-cum-museum of Thomas Mann (*Rašytojo T. Mano Kultūros Centras*). The writer built it on his first visit when he fell in love with the place. He had time to visit only for two summers before having to leave Germany in 1933. Newspaper cuttings and old photos illustrated the context of the times.

Further south, the 19th-century German Lutheran church is surrounded by a cemetery with remarkable carved wooden crosses *(krikštai)*, differing according to the age and gender of the deceased.

Opposite, the Amber Gallery *(Gintaro Galerika-muziejus)* displays Stone Age amulets, pieces of unpolished amber and carved jewels. Also worth a visit is the Fisherman's House *(Žvejo etnografinė sodyba)*.

In the harbour, several traditional fishing boats *(kurėnai)* offer cruises around the lagoon. You may prefer to hire a bicycle and take a ride under the pines and along the promenade leading to the billowing sand dunes. A stairway of 180 steps leads up the Parnidis, the longest dune in the park extending 7 km over the Russian frontier. At the foot of the great granite solar clock standing on the dune, you get a superb view over the village, dunes, lagoon and Baltic.

Regional Park

On the other side of the lagoon, the River Nemunas flows into a vast delta, protected since 1997 by a regional park that covers 350 sq km. This maze of islands, channels, forests, mud pools and meadows that flood at the end of winter and in spring is a cherished haven for waterfowl and other migratory birds. Many gather on the big flat island of Rusnė. Here the storks are all over the place, about as many as there are houses outside the main township.

On the other side of the delta, a lighthouse and ornithological centre (which houses a museum) stand side by side at Ventė Ragas. This windswept spit of land is located at the meeting point of several migratory routes, making it an ideal place for the ornithologists to tag the birds with identifying rings.

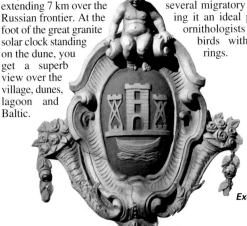

Klaipėda: coat of arms on the façade of a house near the Exchange Bridge (Birzos tiltas).

Dining Out

For starters, the choice generally wavers between smoked eel; cod's liver fritters; salmon roe, the so-called "red caviar" (*raudona ikra*), delicious on blinis; or herring (*silkė*), smoked or marinated, served with hot or cold potatoes and sour cream, onions and sometimes walnuts. You can always order a salad (*salotos*) of mushrooms (*grybai*), cabbage (*kopūstų*), tomatoes and cucumbers, with a dressing often on the thick side. In summer, go for the good cold *šaltibarščiai* soup of red beetroot, egg, dill and cream, served with potatoes.

The most common meat dishes are pork chops (*kotletas*), grilled pork (*karbonadas*), Caucasian shashlik (*šašlykas*), kebabs of grilled beef, chicken, and so on, spicy veal (*veršiena*) in red wine or stuffed (*zrazy*), stuffed cabbage rolls (*balandėliai*), and a kind of ravioli (*koldūnai*) stuffed with meat or mushrooms. Beef tongue (*liežuvis*) is much appreciated cold as a starter or boiled and served with a sauce.

Fish dishes include carp, grilled salmon (*kepta lašiša*), perch or grilled trout (*keptas upėtakis*).

Potatoes accompany most meals and can take many guises.

Blynai are potato cakes spread with sour cream (*su grietine*); they may be flavoured with herring, mushrooms or ham. *Vėdarai* are a kind of potato sausage, *cepelinai* ("zeppelins") are potato dumplings stuffed with meat, while *bulviu, plokštainis* or *kugelis* is a baked potato pudding eaten with apple sauce, sour cream or crumbled fried bacon. Another popular vegetable is the cabbage.

Pancakes (*blynelai* or *lietinai*) may be served as dessert, but they can also constitute a main dish. Savoury versions are made with cream, ham or cheese (*su kumpiu ir sūriu*), mushrooms (*su grybais*); sweet with bananas (*su bananais*), apples (*su obuolčais*), often accompanied by yoghurt, sometimes with a chocolate sauce. There is also a plentiful choice of pastries, ice cream and red fruit jellies thickened with potato flour.

Drinks

Beer (*alus*), good and cheap, vodka, mead (*midus*—fermented honey) or sweet wines are all served with the meal. Mineral water (*mineralinis vanduo*) is also available, as are tea (*arbata*) and coffee (*kava*).